THE GREATEST SHOWMAN ON EARTH

A Biography of P. T. Barnum

By Ann Tompert

P DILLON PRESS, INC.
d Minneapolis, Minnesota 55415

Photographic Acknowledgments

The photographs are reproduced through the courtesy of the Barnum Museum, Bridgeport, Connecticut; the Bettmann Archive; Circus World Museum, Baraboo, Wisconsin; the Theatre Collection, Museum of the City of New York; and Tufts University Archives, Wessell Library.

Library of Congress Cataloging in Publication Data

Tompert, Ann.
  The greatest showman on earth.

  (People in focus)
  Bibliography: p.
  Includes index.
  Summary: A biography of the showman who, among other achievements, created a three-ring circus known as "the greatest show on earth" and was active in Connecticut politics.
    1. Barnum, P.T. (Phineas Taylor), 1810-1891—Juvenile literature.   2. Circus owners—United States—Biography—Juvenile literature.   [1. Barnum, P.T. (Phineas Taylor), 1810-1891.
2. Circus owners]   I. Title.   II. Series.
  GV1811.B3T66   1987 791.3'092'4   [B] [92] 87-13600
  ISBN 0-87518-370-0

Dillon Press, Inc., 242 Portland Avenue South
Minneapolis, Minnesota 55415

Printed in the United States of America
   2 3 4 5 6 7 8 9 10 96 95 94 93 92 91 90 89 88

Contents

Chapter/One

The truth flashed upon me

It was 1881, and the torchlit streets of New York City were ablaze with life and color. An unending stream of dazzling golden chariots drawn by teams of horses, zebras, and deer swept past the half million people jamming the parade route. Cages holding leopards, hyenas, and serpents rolled along, followed by elephants, camels, and horses. Brightly costumed circus performers waved to the crowd. Four brass bands played gaily as they proudly announced the arrival of the greatest show on earth—the Barnum and London Circus!

Over nine thousand spectators filled Madison Square Garden for the first three-ring circus. The pageantry sparkled and glittered under the new electric lights. An eight-foot tall giant named Chang-Yu Sing stood next to the tiny midgets General Tom Thumb and his wife Lavinia. A "two-headed girl"

danced while Japanese jugglers performed their amazing tricks. Daredevil trapeze artists swung through the
air and high-wire artists balanced overhead. So many
thrilling acts filled the three rings that the excited
crowd hardly knew where to look. Children felt as
though they had been transported to a dreamland.
P.T. Barnum had shown once and for all that he was
indeed "The Children's Friend."

Although P.T. Barnum is best known as the creator of the modern circus, he had actually spent sixty
years of his life on other activities before turning his
energies to the circus. As proprietor of Barnum's
American Museum in New York City, he introduced
the Fejee Mermaid, trained dogs, the tiny General
Tom Thumb, the original Siamese twins, and Jenny
Lind to the American public. He brought Jumbo, the
largest elephant in the world, to the United States. To
publicize his attractions, Barnum thought up unusual
advertisements and stunts, earning himself the nick-
name "The Shakespeare of Advertising." He took an
active part in politics. He, over the course of his life,
made, lost, and remade several fortunes.

Barnum loved a good joke and delighted in the art
of humbuggery—playing tricks and hoaxes on people.
He thought of himself as the greatest trickster of them
all and called himself the "Prince of Humbugs." His
elaborate jokes fooled thousands at a time, and they
enjoyed the pranks as much as he did. Barnum had
found that people did not mind being tricked as long

HUM - BUG.

P.T. Barnum called himself the "Prince of Humbugs." A cartoonist of the time drew this humorous picture of Barnum as the "Hum-Bug."

as they were entertained in the bargain. Barnum's famous hoaxes and publicity stunts, the variety of attractions at the American Museum, and the shows he sponsored throughout the world made him America's first showman—and finally, the creator of the greatest show on earth.

Phineas Taylor Barnum was born July 5, 1810, in Bethel, Connecticut. Abraham Lincoln had been born just one year earlier and the United States had been an independent country for only thirty-four years. Phineas Taylor was the oldest of five children of Philo Barnum and his second wife, Irene Taylor. Philo's first wife had died, leaving five children. As was common then in New England, he remarried within six months, partly to give a mother to his children. Phineas Taylor Barnum was named after his mother's father, Phineas Taylor, who adored his grandson. In turn, young Taylor, as he was called, worshipped his grandfather. Grandfather Taylor kept him supplied with lumps of sugar and gave him pennies to buy candy and raisins. Grandfather Taylor also began young Taylor's lessons in Yankee thrift, telling his grandson to bargain with the storekeeper for the best possible cash price.

Taylor learned this lesson so well that he began to save his money before he was five years old. By the time he was six, Taylor had gathered enough pennies to exchange them for a silver dollar. Many years later, he recalled that this silver dollar, his first, made him feel far richer than he had ever felt since.

From then on, Taylor continued to be on the lookout for ways to make money. He was only eight or nine when he earned ten cents for every one hundred horns of cattle, sheep, goats, and other animals he prepared for the small comb factories in Bethel. He had to scrape out the bony material inside the horns, leaving the outside to be cut and shaped into combs.

On holidays, instead of spending money, he earned it. He peddled homemade molasses candy, gingerbread cookies, and cherry rum, which he made by adding sugar and the juice of wild cherries to New England rum.

"I generally found myself a dollar or two richer at the end of the holiday...," he said. "By the time I was twelve years old, besides other property, I was the owner of a sheep and a calf." He would have been richer, he added, had not his father "kindly" let him buy his own clothes.

Most of Taylor's time was spent helping his father with the farm. Every morning he took the cows to pasture where they ate grass all day. Every night he brought them home to be milked. He hoed and weeded the garden and helped gather hay. "And as I grew older," he said, "I earned ten cents a day riding the horse which led the ox-team in plowing."

Taylor attended the Bethel district school from the time he was six until he was twelve years old. Like many farm children of the time, however, he was not able to attend regularly. Taylor dreaded the schoolhouse and was terrified of his schoolmaster, who kept order by whipping his pupils with a ruler or a birch rod. Later, he said that he deserved and received his share of this kind of punishment.

Although Taylor thought his teachers were better at keeping order than teaching, he was a good student, especially in arithmetic. In fact, he was so good that one night he was called out of bed by his teacher, who had bet a neighbor that Taylor could figure out in five minutes the correct number of feet in a load of lumber. He did it in two, using the stovepipe in the kitchen to write on. Taylor was often taken from school to help on the farm, but his mother, true to her Puritan beliefs, allowed nothing to keep him from attending the Sunday church meeting.

Everyone was expected to support and attend the Puritan Sunday church services whether they were Puritans or not. Those who did not were fined. Those who did attend spent the morning in a bare meeting house saying prayers and listening to a sermon. After a dinner break at noon, several more hours were spent in the same way. There was no music and the unheated meeting houses were unbearably cold in winter.

Like other children, Taylor spent the day with his parents in church, visiting family and friends, or reading the Bible and other religious books. Above all, he was expected to be quiet! Long before he could read, Taylor became known as a good student in Sunday school. His mother listened to his lessons and helped him win a reward of merit. She also taught Taylor to fear the everlasting fires of hell.

At the beginning of the nineteenth century, many Puritan ideas and attitudes influenced not just Connecticut but all the New England states. In the seventeenth century the Puritans left England seeking religious freedom. They settled in New England and set up communities where Puritan ministers had a great influence in government matters and government officials had a large measure of control over church affairs. By the early 1800s, the Puritans had lost their power over the government. But the churches they established, including the Congregationalist church the Barnums attended, still affected people's lives.

To the Puritans, hard work was a religious duty. It was against the law to cook, make beds, sweep floors, cut hair, or shave on Sunday. Young people were fined if they ran or jumped or sang on that day. Wasting time on amusements was considered sinful. Christmas was treated as an ordinary day. Shows or theaters of any kind were forbidden by law. Dancing and card-playing were not allowed. Anyone who swore was fined. If offenders were not fined, they could be punished by a public whipping or jailed. Jail also awaited people who did not pay their debts.

Except for the weather, each day was very much

like the one before in Puritan New England. Perhaps because they realized that they needed something to relieve the boredom of their day-to-day lives, the Puritans did not object to the playing of practical jokes. And Grandfather Taylor was a master of the art. "My grandfather," Taylor said, "would go farther, wait longer, work harder, contrive deeper, to carry out a practical joke than for anything else under the sun."

And even though he loved his grandson, Grandfather Taylor had made young Taylor the victim of one of his most elaborate jokes. When Taylor was born, his grandfather gave him the deed to a five-acre piece of land called Ivy Island. Throughout the years, Taylor's family and friends told him he was the richest child in Bethel because he owned one of the most valuable farms in Connecticut. He was convinced that it had caverns of diamonds and mines of silver and gold. By the time he was ten, Taylor had grown so eager to see his property that he pestered his father into agreeing that the time had come at last.

Yet when he finally stepped onto his island, Taylor saw nothing but a few stunted ivies and straggling trees. "The truth flashed upon me," he said. "I had been the laughingstock of the family and neighbors for years." It was his first and last visit to Ivy Island.

Although Grandfather Taylor's hoax seemed cruel, perhaps he was trying to give young Taylor such a lesson that he would never be fooled again. Being as clever as he was, Taylor might have understood this, although he was hurt and humiliated at the time.

When Taylor was twelve, he helped a farmer drive some cattle from Bethel to New York City to sell. His mother gave him a dollar for spending money. After buying some oranges, which were a rare treat in those days, he visited a toy shop. What delightful things it was filled with! He completely forgot his lessons in Yankee thrift. He bought a toy gun. The next day he got some firecrackers. On the third day he bought a watch and a top. The following day, he went back and saw a beautiful knife with two blades and a corkscrew for thirty-one cents. Though he only had eleven cents left, he persuaded the shopkeeper to exchange the top and the eleven cents for the knife.

Then some fine and nearly white molasses candy caught his eye. He thought it must be something very special since the molasses candy he usually ate was dark brown. He just had to try some, so he traded the watch for a few pieces of the candy. It was so delicious that before nightfall he had traded his toy gun for more candy. The next morning his firecrackers were traded. And before that night his knife was gone too. Still, his sweet tooth was not satisfied. He traded the two extra handkerchiefs and an extra pair of stockings he had brought with him from home for more of the wonderful candy.

When he returned to Bethel, his brothers and sisters were disappointed because he did not bring them any gifts from New York. And when his mother found two pocket handkerchiefs and one pair of stockings missing, she whipped him and sent him to bed. That was his first experience in swapping, one he always remembered.

Although he worked from an early age, Taylor felt that the farm was no place for him. "I always disliked working with my hands," he said. He enjoyed using his head, however, and was always ready to make plans for fun or earning money.

Taylor's father worried about him. How would Taylor earn his living if he did not want to farm or do any kind of work with his hands? He decided that the only solution was to make a merchant out of his son. So, Philo Barnum put up a building in Bethel and took on another man as partner. He purchased a stock of dry goods, hardware, groceries, and general notions such as buttons, lace, ribbons, needles, handkerchiefs, stockings, combs, buckles, and beads. At the age of twelve, Taylor became the clerk of this country store.

He hated taking down the shutters, sweeping the floor, and making a fire because he felt that these jobs were not dignified enough for him. But he enjoyed the "head-work" needed to run a business where some people paid cash and some bought on credit. Most customers, however, bartered or traded the things they had made or grown for goods they needed from the Barnum store. He drove hard bargains with the women who brought butter, eggs, bees-wax, and feathers to exchange for dry goods, and with the men who wanted to trade oats and other items for tenpenny nails, molasses, or New England rum.

While clerking, Taylor sometimes found stones, gravel, or ashes in a bundle of material that a housewife claimed was cotton and linen. Sometimes a farmer gave short measure on a load of oats or corn or rye. Because he was bright, Taylor usually managed to avoid being taken in by these schemes, but his experience at the store taught him a great deal about tricks, dishonesty, and deception.

Taylor received a small salary for his services. To that he added what profit he could make from buying candy with his own money and selling it to his younger customers.

There were times for fun, too. In the evenings and on rainy or snowy days, business was always slow. Then the village pranksters gathered in the store for story-telling and joke-playing. Like others of the time, his mother frowned on amusement of any sort as sinful, so Taylor frequently spent his free evenings at the homes of other village boys, where he enjoyed hearing more tales.

Besides farming and owning a country store, Taylor's father worked as a tailor occasionally, kept a tavern and hotel of sorts, had a livery stable, and ran a small express service that carried merchandise from Bethel to the surrounding towns. Taylor felt that under different circumstances, his father might have been a successful man. Yet he never managed to make a profit in any of his businesses. However, Taylor saw his father's energy and thought that perhaps he had that same enterprising spirit himself.

When Taylor was fifteen, his father died, leaving five children still at home—the youngest of them was seven years old. He had left no money to take care of his family. His estate was bankrupt. Taylor had loaned all his savings to his father, and this was also lost to creditors. He was forced to buy the pair of shoes that he wore to his father's funeral on credit. Taylor could truly say that he began his adult life with nothing, and was barefooted at that.

Chapter Two

My proper position was not yet reached

After his father's death in 1825, Barnum tried many things to earn a living. His first job was clerking for James Keeler and Lewis Whitlock in Grassy Plains, a small town about a mile away from Bethel. He earned six dollars a month and his meals. His employers soon learned that he was a shrewd trader and allowed him to make deals for them. They also let him conduct business for himself on the side.

One day, while the owners were away, Barnum traded some tinware, which had been sitting on the store shelves many years, for a load of green glass bottles of various sizes and shapes. "You have made a fool of yourself," said Mr. Keeler when he returned, "for you have enough bottles here to supply the whole town for twenty years."

Barnum decided that a lottery could prove his employer wrong. At the time, lotteries were legal and easy to operate. A sponsor sold numbered tickets. Buyers had a chance to win prizes if their numbers were drawn from among all the numbers sold. The sponsor kept part of the money received from the sale of the tickets and put the rest into prizes. Some sponsors offered merchandise as prizes while others awarded money. Sponsors of lotteries often paid agents to sell tickets for them. Barnum had learned all about lotteries from his Grandfather Taylor, who was an agent for one.

In his lottery, Barnum sold one thousand tickets, offering five hundred prizes in goods from the store. The first prize winner could choose twenty-five dollars worth of merchandise. The other winners had to take what Barnum selected. Of course, most of the winners ended up with green glass bottles and the rest of the leftover tinware. In less than two weeks, Barnum cleared the store of bottles and unwanted utensils.

In 1827 Keeler and Whitlock sold their business and Barnum went to Brooklyn, New York, to clerk in a grocery store owned by a distant relative. He lived above the store in a room on the third floor. Barnum did not like to get up early, but he did not want to miss any customers either, so he tied a string to his big toe and asked the night watchman to tug at the string when the first buyer appeared.

Barnum managed the store successfully and was treated well by his employer. But he was not satisfied.

Just working for a salary was not enough. He felt he needed to be in business for himself, where his profits would depend on his own efforts. He quit his job, took the money he had earned, and opened a porter-house—a tavern—where he sold beer by the glass. After a few short months he sold out at a profit. Then he became a bartender in another porterhouse.

After he had been away from Bethel for a year or so, Barnum's mother and Grandfather Taylor were eager to have him back home. His grandfather even offered him his carriage house rent-free to lure him back. So in February of 1828, Barnum returned to Bethel to start a fruit and candy store.

His store opened for business on the first Monday in May. It was Spring Training Day, when all the men from the surrounding area gathered for a day of military training and drills. Barnum knew he was guaranteed a good crowd of people. In that one day, he made back his entire investment—less seven dollars. Going to New York, he reinvested his money in more fruits and candy. To these he added "fancy goods" such as pocketbooks, combs, beads, rings, pocketknives, and toys. At the suggestion of Grandfather Taylor, he also became an agent for a state-wide lottery. As agent he kept 10 percent of the money he took in for himself.

His business was so successful that he decided it was finally time to ask Charity Hallet if she would marry him. He had loved her since he was sixteen, when he was a clerk at the Grassy Plains store. They had met when Charity, who was a tailoress in Bethel, visited Grassy Plains one Saturday afternoon to buy a hat at the milliner's. A violent storm came up, and Charity was afraid to ride her horse alone the mile home to Bethel. The milliner, knowing that Barnum always went home on Saturday to spend Sunday with his family, asked him to see Charity home safely.

Soon after they started on their way, Barnum found himself falling in love and wishing that the distance to Bethel were twenty miles instead of just one. Barnum saw Charity at church the next day and on many Sundays after that. He also saw her at house-raisings, corn-huskings, apple-parings, and other community affairs. In keeping with the times, he seldom saw her alone, but he did manage occasionally to take her on a buggy ride or on a sleigh ride with his grandfather's horse and a sleigh. Both families objected to their marriage. Barnum's mother thought the twenty-one-year-old Charity was too old for her nineteen-year-old son. She also thought that Barnum was too important a person to be marrying a tailoress. Charity's family and friends, on the other hand, thought that she was too good for Barnum.

The young couple decided to get married secretly. In October 1829, Charity went to New York to visit her uncle. Saying he needed supplies for his store, Barnum followed her there early in November. On November 8, 1829, Barnum became, he said, "the husband of one of the best women in America." At first, Barnum's mother was angry at his secret marriage, but she soon invited him to bring his wife to Sunday dinner, a sign that all was forgiven.

Soon after his marriage, Barnum built a two-and-a-half story home for his bride. He also built a three-story building. On the ground floor, he opened a general store with an uncle, while the other two floors had apartments to rent.

The next three years were busy ones for Barnum. Besides keeping his store in Bethel, he opened lottery offices in Danbury, Norwalk, Stamford, and several other villages within a thirty-mile radius. He often sold two thousand dollars worth of tickets a day, a small fortune. There were other agents selling tickets, but Barnum persuaded people to buy from him by advertising. He covered his lottery offices with large gold signs and brightly colored posters and passed out handbills describing the fortunes to be made by buying his lottery tickets. This was the beginning of advertising as it is known today. Barnum was the first one to use advertising and publicity campaigns to stir people's imaginations and interest in his business projects.

On his twenty-first birthday, Barnum gained the right to vote and with it an interest in politics. He saw what he thought was a dangerous development. He felt that church leaders were mixing too much into governmental matters and wrote several articles expressing this opinion. The nearest newspaper, in Danbury, refused to publish them, saying they were too controversial.

This did not stop Barnum. He liked nothing better than stirring up arguments. On October 19, 1831, he became owner, editor, and publisher of his own newspaper, *The Herald of Freedom*, in which he opposed anything which took away the liberties of the people or any actions he considered unjust. This four-page journal was published every Wednesday and cost two dollars a year, delivered to the door.

Several people accused him of libel, saying he deliberately tried to ruin their good names. Some even took him to court. Barnum had accused a minister of cheating an orphan out of some money. Although he had written the truth, he had used what the judge considered unsuitable language. The judge found Barnum guilty, fined him one hundred dollars, and sent him off to jail for sixty days.

Barnum published 160 issues of *The Herald of Freedom* under his name. Then he began to have money problems so he turned it over to his brother-in-law. Although the paper was not a financial success, Barnum gained valuable experience. He had an inborn sense of what made a good news story and all the talents to become an excellent journalist if he had wanted that career.

For several years after his marriage, Barnum seemed to be very successful, but in 1834 he had to admit that he was a failure. His store was no longer making money. He had bought supplies in large amounts to get them cheaper. But Barnum found that he had been too generous in giving credit when he sold these goods. His customers owed him money that they could not or would not pay. To add to his problems, the state of Connecticut passed a law forbidding lotteries. His one good source of income dried up when he was forced to close all his lottery offices.

Barnum decided there was nothing left for him in Bethel. In the winter of 1834 he sold everything he owned. Then, after hiring an agent to collect the money still owed him from bad debts, he moved to New York City with his wife and newborn daughter, Caroline.

At this time New York had a population of about two hundred thousand. Its people loved amusement, and the Barnums found it much livelier than Connecticut. But New York, like the rest of the country, was suffering a financial depression. The year that Barnum arrived, the city was almost destroyed by a large fire. More than seven hundred buildings were destroyed. Many companies went out of business, and banks could not pay their depositors. There were few opportunities to make money.

Living on what little savings he had, Barnum spent the whole winter looking for work without finding anything. Finally, in the spring he received several hundred dollars from his agent in Bethel.

With this money he opened a small private boarding house on May 1, 1835, because he could find no better business. He placed an advertisement in Connecticut newspapers and was soon playing host to his many friends who visited New York for business or pleasure. This did not keep him busy enough, however, so with a partner he bought a grocery store. Once more Barnum was earning a fair living, but he was not satisfied.

"By this time," he said, "it was clear to my mind that my proper position in this busy world was not yet reached. The business for which I was destined, and, I believe, made, had not come to me."

Chapter/Three

The most astonishing curiosity in the world

Barnum's career in show business started with a hoax. In 1835, although he still managed his grocery store in New York, he was bored and dissatisfied with his job. He continued to look for something more interesting and exciting. One day, Coley Bartram, an acquaintance from Connecticut, told him about Joice Heth, who was on exhibit in Philadelphia.

At that time, it was common practice for showmen to exhibit curiosities in display rooms. People saw nothing wrong with paying a small fee to see a two-headed cow, a six-legged dog, a legless man, an armless woman, a dwarf, a giant, or other people and animals that were considered unusual. Showmen often made their livings managing exhibits like these. Most traveled from town to town, producing shows that might include human or animal displays, artwork, acrobats, or perhaps even a small circus. And, in 1835 slavery was still legal in the United States. Joice Heth was being presented to the public as a 161-year-old slave who was nurse to George Washington when he was a baby.

As Bartram talked, ideas raced through Barnum's head. He was shown a bill of sale for Joice Heth dated February 5, 1727. It stated that she was 54 years old at that time. When Barnum saw her lying on a bed, he thought she looked as if she could have been far older than 161. She was blind and no longer had any teeth. She could not straighten her legs or one arm. However, she was very alert, and would talk about "dear little George" as long as she had interested listeners. Sometimes she talked about religious subjects or sang an old hymn.

Satisfied as to Joice Heth's age, Barnum decided to buy her without any further proof than the bill of sale he had been shown. Although the asking price was three thousand dollars, Barnum soon bargained it down to one thousand dollars. Since he actually had only five hundred dollars, he borrowed five hundred, sold his interest in the grocery business to his partner, and began the life of a showman.

Barnum was convinced that his success in exhibiting Joice Heth depended upon publicity. He had to get everyone thinking, talking, and excited about her. So, shortly after he bought Joice, he began flooding New York City with handbills and posters carrying her picture. In his publicity pieces, Barnum described

Joice as "the most astonishing and interesting curiosity in the world." He held his first public showing in rented rooms and persuaded the newspapers to publish stories and favorable reviews of his exhibit of George Washington's nurse.

After a profitable New York show, Barnum took Joice on a tour of New England, but the attendance began to fall off there. To rekindle interest, Barnum wrote a letter to the local newspaper. He signed it "A Visitor," and said that Joice Heth was a fraud—that she was a machine made up of whalebone, molded rubber, and hidden springs. Of course, those who had seen Joice before returned to see if they had been fooled, and those who had not seen her now went out of curiosity.

Barnum's successful tour ended after six months upon Joice's death. A medical examination conducted after her death revealed that she could not have been more than eighty years old.

Barnum was accused of fraud. But he maintained then, and throughout the rest of his life, that he had bought Joice and exhibited her in good faith; that it was he who had been tricked. Hoaxed or not, after the experience Barnum said, "I [have] at last found my true vocation."

In his next scheme, Barnum hired a man called Signor Antonio who did balancing stunts, stilt-walking, plate-spinning, and other remarkable tricks. He even fired a gun at a target while hopping on one ten-foot-high stilt! Barnum changed Antonio's name to Signor Vivalla because he thought Antonio did not sound foreign enough. Then, Barnum advertised that this amazing acrobat had just arrived from Italy, since he knew people were always more interested in seeing a foreign peformer than an American one. Because the United States was still a young country, its people had not yet developed their own ideas about what was worthwhile in entertainment and the arts. They were so unsure of their own tastes and opinions that American writers, painters, singers, musicians, and other artists were almost always rejected as inferior to those who came from England or Europe.

As he had done with Joice Heth, Barnum tried to make sure that everyone in New York had heard of Signor Vivalla. His efforts led to a profitable stay in New York. Then, he sent his wife and daughter Caroline back home to Bethel and accompanied Signor Vivalla on a successful tour of Boston, Philadelphia, and Washington, D.C.

Soon after this, Barnum and Signor Vivalla joined Aaron Turner's traveling circus. Barnum served as ticket-taker, secretary, and treasurer at thirty dollars a month plus one-fifth of all the profits. In the summer of 1836, they toured the villages and towns of New England, New York, New Jersey, Pennsylvania, Delaware, Virginia, and North Carolina.

The company consisted of three dozen men, nine horses, and four wagons. The bandsmen put up the

tent and the performers made the ring. Two of Turner's sons did tricks with horses. Along with Signor
Vivalla, the acts included a clown, a song and dance
man, a magician, and some musicians. In order to
make as much profit as he could, Turner was very
careful about how he spent money. One time while
the company was traveling, it stopped for lunch along
the road. Turner fed the whole group with food he
bought at a farmhouse for fifty cents.

Turner managed so well that when Barnum sepa-
rated from the circus in October of 1836, he took
twelve hundred dollars with him. And he had learned
the business well enough to start his own traveling
circus called Barnum's Grand Scientific and Musical
Theatre. The acts were constantly changing as people
joined for a while and then left. The usual performers
were Signor Vivalla, the acrobat; Joe Pentland, a com-
bination clown, ventriloquist, comic singer, and acrobat; James Sandford, a black singer and dancer; and
several musicians. With these performers, his horses
and wagons, and a small tent, Barnum started on a
tour of the South.

In March of 1838, the group reached New Or-
leans where they performed for a week. In June,
Signor Vivalla retired to Cuba, and Barnum decided
it was time to return home. He exchanged the steam-
boat for sugar and molasses, which he sold. The company disbanded. Barnum returned to New York and
brought his family back from Bethel.

Barnum had made twenty-five hundred dollars, a nice profit, but he was not satisfied. He was eager to find a business that would give him a steady income, so he advertised that he had money to invest. He received ninety-three answers, a third of them from porterhouse keepers. Most of the rest came from pawnbrokers, lottery dealers, patent medicine men, and inventors. Probably the most daring and shameless suggestion came from a counterfeiter who showed Barnum some fake paper money. He wanted two thousand dollars to make some new dies (the metal plates used in printing money) and to buy paper and ink. He promised to make Barnum rich if he joined him in the business of printing bogus dollars.

In the spring of 1839, Barnum finally formed a partnership with a German named Proler, who manufactured a waterproof polish for black boots; a paste called bear's grease for keeping leather soft; and cologne water, a kind of perfume. At first the company seemed to prosper, but a year and a half later it failed. The partners were in debt. Barnum's money was gone. Proler had agreed to buy the business from Barnum for twenty-six hundred dollars, but then ran off to the Netherlands without paying the money. Barnum was left with a handful of worthless receipts.

Barnum's funds were dangerously low. He had a family to support. He dreaded going back to the life of a traveling showman, but there seemed to be nothing else to do. Although he was discouraged, Barnum still had faith that somehow all would work out to his benefit. He decided to go on the road again. Once more he sent his wife and family back to Bethel. Then, scraping together one hundred dollars, he gathered a small company of entertainers—a singer, a dancer, and a fiddler—and set out. They toured for eight months with only moderate success and returned to New York in April of 1841. After this experience Barnum resolved never again to be a traveling showman.

Chapter/Four

They speak too well of you

When Barnum returned from his eight-month road trip in 1841, he was thirty-one years old. He had a wife and two children, Caroline and Helen, to support. Soon he would have three children. Yet, he was no better off financially than he had been when he first arrived in New York five years earlier. It was at this time that he read an advertisement for *Sears' Pictorial Illustrations of the Bible*, published by Robert Sears.

Convinced that he could mend his fortunes, Barnum decided to invest all his money, five hundred dollars, in Sears' project. For this he received five hundred copies of the book and an agency for its sale throughout the United States. He opened an office in New York, advertised widely, and in six months sold several thousand copies of the book. Then he decided to expand, hiring men to sell the book in other cities. These agents were not trustworthy and cheated him so badly that he lost all his profits and his original investment as well. For the second time, Barnum had trusted the wrong people. It was not to be the last. But he never lost his faith in people.

Once more Barnum was broke and forced to scratch for a living. He wrote theater advertisements for four dollars a week, and he composed articles for the Sunday papers. "I was glad," he said, "to do anything that would keep the wolf from the door."

Barnum was always optimistic. No matter how bad things were, he was always sure that his affairs would improve. And improve they did. He was clerking for a theater when he learned that Scudder's American Museum was for sale at a price of fifteen thousand dollars. He was determined to buy it because he was convinced that the museum would offer him an opportunity to make money quickly.

At that time in New York, amusements were limited. There was no Metropolitan Museum of Art, no American Museum of Natural History, and no Zoological Gardens. The theaters generally had bad reputations. The plays presented were frequently in bad taste and often used vulgar language. Bad-mannered and rowdy people often spent a great deal of time in theaters. Those who valued their good names would never risk being seen in these places of amusement.

There were two or three theaters that were acceptable to the general public. But even those were not patronized by people who still held a Puritan belief that entertainment of any kind was sinful. They were convinced that theaters were managed by the devil.

Scudder's American Museum and similar places that had exhibits and lecture halls were about the only places that people felt they could find acceptable entertainment. The proprietors did not present their attractions only to entertain but also to teach. If audiences went to a lecture room to see an acrobat, a lady magician, or a tattooed man, surely there was no harm if they had a bit of fun along with the education. Of course, Barnum had his own view of the matter. "Men, women, and children," he declared, "cannot always be serious. They need something to satisfy their lighter moments."

With the museum, Barnum planned to fill that need. When he told his plan to a friend who knew that Barnum was living from hand to mouth, the friend asked him what he intended to buy the museum with. "Brass," Barnum replied, "for silver and gold have I none."

Barnum's plan was a bold one. He wrote a letter to Francis Olmsted, the owner of the building that housed the collection. He suggested that Olmsted sell him the collection on credit. Then, except for six hundred dollars a year which Barnum would use to support his family, Olmsted would receive all the profits until the collection was paid for. In addition, Barnum would pay twenty-five hundred dollars a year rent for the building plus five hundred dollars a year for a billiard room in the building that Olmsted owned next door to the museum. This Barnum would convert to an apartment for his wife and family. "If at any time," he wrote, "I fail to meet the installments due, I will vacate the premises and forfeit all that might have been paid to that date."

Olmsted agreed to talk with Barnum about his proposal. At that meeting, he asked for references— people who could discuss Barnum's character and business ability. Barnum's friends on the New York newspapers and in show business all spoke very highly of him. But when Olmsted and Barnum met again a few days later Olmsted said he did not like these references. There was a puzzled look on Barnum's face and he said he was sorry. He wondered where he could get better ones. He saw his dream slipping away and his heart sank.

"They speak too well of you," Olmsted said. Then he laughed! "In fact, they all talk as if they were partners of yours and intended to share the profits."

Barnum sighed with relief. But then Olmsted asked him if he owned any unmortgaged property to put up as security. Barnum had nothing. He saw his dream slipping away again. But then he remembered Ivy Island and that day nineteen years before when Grandfather Taylor had played a practical joke on him. Couldn't he play the same joke on Olmsted? It would do no harm, as Barnum knew he could make a success of the museum if he had a chance. He told

Olmsted about the five acres his grandfather had given him. He let Olmsted believe that it was a valuable piece of property, and that he cherished it as a gift from his beloved Grandfather Taylor. Olmsted accepted his proposal, giving Barnum the last laugh over Ivy Island. After some delay caused by a rival buyer, Barnum bought the American Museum's collection in Olmsted's name for twelve thousand dollars instead of the asking price of fifteen thousand dollars.

Barnum opened the museum under his management at sunrise on New Year's Day, 1842. From then on, the doors were open each day at dawn. Out-of-towners who arrived early in the morning often visited it before going to their hotels. Families brought their lunches and ate them at the museum so they could spend the whole day viewing its attractions.

From the day he opened the museum, Barnum was determined to make it a success. He worked to mold it into the most popular and attractive place of entertainment in the United States. The building housed a valuable collection when he bought it, including stuffed animals and snakes, historic flags, military uniforms, guns, medals, old coins, unusual shells, portraits of famous Americans, wax figures of famous heroes and villains, models of Jerusalem and Paris, and hundreds of other exhibits. There were also living animals and people. Among them could be found a dog that played cards and dominoes and a twenty-year-old midget who was only thirty-nine inches tall.

Although the collection was so big that no one could see it all in one day, Barnum began to add more attractions immediately. He introduced to the public an armless man, models of European landscapes and biblical scenes, an albino woman, a tatooed man, dwarfs, ropedancers, and many other curiosities.

Barnum also enlarged the lecture hall. Scudder usually had a professor giving a talk on some scientific or geographic topic every evening. Occasionally there was a matinee. Once in a while he had an acrobat or some other act. Barnum knew he had to have more excitement than that if he wanted to keep his patrons coming back again and again.

He scoured the country for unusual acts to present in the lecture hall so that he always had something new to offer.

Although Barnum was openhanded when spending money on his museum, he was economical when it came to providing for his family. Besides housing Charity and their daughters Caroline, Helen, and Frances, next door to the museum, he supported them on six hundred dollars a year. This was less than two dollars a day, not very much when it cost fifty cents for three loaves of bread and a pound of butter. As small as this amount was, Barnum said, "My treasure of a wife was willing to reduce this sum to four hundred dollars if necessary."

Charity had grown up in poverty and, like her husband, had the Yankee spirit of thrift. Yet it was a struggle to feed and clothe two adults and three children on such a small amount. However, she did not complain. She did what had to be done even though she was already beginning to suffer the poor health which would remain with her for the rest of her life.

A few months after Barnum took over the museum, Olmsted stopped by the ticket office at noon. For his dinner, his main meal of the day, Barnum was eating cold corned beef and bread, which he had brought from home. When Olmsted questioned him about it, Barnum replied, "I have not eaten a warm dinner except on Sundays since I bought the museum, and I never intend to, on a weekday, till I am out of debt."

"You. . .will pay for the museum before the year is out," said Olmsted.

And he was right. In less than a year, Barnum owned the American Museum collection in his own name, and he had paid his rent out of his profits of $27,912.62. The year before he had become its proprietor, the museum's profits had been only $10,862.

Chapter/Five

Advertising is like learning

Barnum spent time and money improving the museum's attractions. He expanded the presentations in its lecture room. Then he advertised. He constantly studied ways to attract attention, to startle, to make people talk and wonder. His goal was to keep three words in the public eye—Barnum's American Museum.

Barnum spent the entire profits of his first year on keeping the public aware of his name and that of his museum. "Advertising is like learning," he said. "A little is a dangerous thing. . . . A reader of a newspaper does not see the first insertion of an ordinary advertisement; the second one he sees but does not read; the third one he reads; the fourth one he looks at the price; the fifth one he speaks to his wife; the sixth one he is ready to buy; the seventh he buys."

Barnum discovered some new ways to get people interested in his exhibits. Much of his success was due to his unusual methods of advertising. "I studied ways. . .to let the world know I had a museum," he declared.

In seeking publicity, Barnum began with the drab, five-story marble building that housed the museum. People passed by every day without noticing it. Then one morning, eyes popped and traffic stopped as everyone stared at the complete change in the building. "I never saw so many open mouths and astonished eyes," Barnum reported. Overnight, the dull structure had become a rainbow of color. Large oval paintings of all kinds of animals had been placed between all the windows of the entire building. Naturally Barnum expected that after seeing the paintings on the outside, people would go inside the museum to see what it had. And he was right. From then on, he took in almost a hundred dollars a day more than before the paintings went up.

Barnum also wanted his building to attract attention at night. When dusk fell, dim lamps flickered on the buildings and streets of New York. It was three years before Thomas Edison would invent the electric light. To draw people to his museum, Barnum installed calcium lights across the top of his building These spotlights were the very first ones seen in New York and were so powerful that they would, Barnum claimed, "enable one to read a newspaper in the street." Every night, like a huge lighted box, the building glowed in the dark streets. Hundreds of people were lured to the museum and, once there, they went on inside, just as Barnum expected they would.

Along with the newly decorated museum, Barnum offered free concerts and kept a band playing on the third floor balcony facing the street. Of course, everyone flocked toward the building to hear the group perform. The musicians were so bad, however, that frequently people hurried inside the museum to escape the noise. "Of course the music was poor," said Barnum. "When people expect something for nothing, they are usually cheated."

Inside, Barnum found ways to drum up even more business. He instituted the baby show and gave prizes for the most beautiful baby, the fattest baby, the handsomest twins, the loveliest triplets, and so on. These were so successful that Barnum later hosted flower, dog, poultry, and bird shows. He created a sensation when he sponsored a "Gallery of Beauty" in which he offered two hundred prizes to "the handsomest women in America." The public voted their choices from daguerreotypes (early types of photographs) that the contestants sent to the museum.

People told their friends about Barnum and his unusual promotions. His fame spread through New York City as more and more people heard about the creative owner of the American Museum. Barnum counted on this word-of-mouth advertising. "It was the best advertisement I could possibly have," he said, "and one for which I could afford to pay."

Many people came to P.T. Barnum's American Museum because of the
imaginative ways in which he publicized its attractions. This 1851
woodcut shows one of Barnum's original posters for "Humbug's
American Museum."

Often Barnum seized upon a promotional opportunity by instinct, even before he knew how he would use it. He had the ability to make the most of chance happenings. One day an unemployed man came by and asked Barnum for a job. Although Barnum agreed to hire the man, he had no idea how he would use him. But he hatched a scheme almost at once. Barnum gave the man five bricks. He told his new worker to lay the first brick on a street corner near the museum, the second brick a bit closer to the museum, the third diagonally across the way from the museum, and the fourth in front of the church that was opposite the museum. "Then," Barnum continued, "with the fifth brick in hand, take a rapid march from one point to the other, making the circuit, exchanging your brick at each point."

At the end of every hour, the man was to enter the museum, walk through every hall in the building, go out again, and resume exchanging bricks. Within half an hour after the man started this routine, five hundred people were watching his mysterious movements. At the end of the first hour, the sidewalks were packed with people. The man ignored these spectators and their questions about his actions.

When he entered the museum, many of the spectators followed, hoping for an answer to his puzzling conduct. The man merely looked about solemnly for fifteen minutes or so, went out, and then started his rounds again.

This routine continued for several days and pulled many visitors into the museum. It ended when the police asked Barnum to call in his "brick man." The great crowds of spectators were causing too many problems.

Barnum was so successful in drawing people that on holidays the museum often became overcrowded. Barnum could not admit any more visitors and had to stop selling tickets. It made him unhappy to look down the street and see hundreds of people being turned away. Something had to be done. Never at a loss for ideas, Barnum quickly had a sign painted that read:

TO THE EGRESS

He placed the sign over a door leading down the back stairs to the outside. The crowds eagerly went through the door and down the stairs, thinking they were on their way to the exhibit of yet another exotic animal. If anyone complained, Barnum assured them that he was not trying to pull another hoax. Why, he thought everyone knew that "egress" was just another word for "exit."

Barnum did not depend solely on advertising and publicity to make all the country aware of the American Museum. He was always on the lookout for bigger and better exhibits. Yet some of his early attractions were hoaxes.

The Fejee Mermaid was one of the most controversial of Barnum's early curiosities. The so-called mermaid actually was a three-foot-long mummified "creature" that had been cleverly constructed from the upper half of a monkey and the lower half of a fish. Its face was ugly and its twisted arms ended in long, crooked fingers. The whole figure was dried up and black.

Barnum suspected that the mermaid was manufactured when he bought it. And he was not sure whether anyone really believed in mermaids. He knew that his first job was to convince people that mermaids truly existed. Then he could persuade them to pay to see his.

After deciding to conceal his connection with the mermaid for a while, Barnum hired a friend to pose as "Dr. Griffin." Dr. Griffin was to pretend to be on his way to London's Lyceum (School) of Natural History with a real mermaid that had been found in the Fiji Islands and preserved.

That arranged, Barnum managed to plant a series of news stories about Dr. Griffin and the Fejee Mermaid in the New York papers. Then Barnum had glamorized pictures of mermaids published. Finally, he printed ten thousand pamphlets on the subject of mermaids. He had newsboys sell these at a penny each in hotels, stores, and other public places.

When he had stirred up enough excitement, Barnum secretly arranged for Dr. Griffin to show his mermaid for one week at Concert Hall in New York City. From the first day, the theater was crowded with people eager to see the mysterious creature. At the end of the week, Barnum announced that he had persuaded Dr. Griffin to exhibit the Fejee Mermaid at his American Museum, where it could be seen at no extra charge. Even without the extra charge, however, Barnum's receipts tripled while the mermaid was on display.

Until that time, only people who lived in New York or visited there knew of the museum and its owner. As a result of the Fejee Mermaid publicity, the American Museum and Barnum were well on their way to being national institutions.

After the excitement from the Fejee Mermaid had died down, Barnum found a new display that again had people lining up at the museum's entrance. For two hundred dollars, Barnum had bought a working model of Niagara Falls, with its surrounding buildings and trees constructed to scale. He advertised it as the "Great Model of the Niagara Falls with Real Water." The real Niagara Falls, on the border between New York State and Canada, was a popular place for honeymooners, but many newlyweds could not afford to go there. They visited Barnum's model instead. They were greatly disappointed when they discovered that the "Great Model" was only eighteen inches high. If the visitors complained, Barnum reminded them that they still got to see the rest of his marvelous museum for their twenty-five cents admission.

Early in his career, Barnum's actions showed again and again that he believed any misrepresentation was acceptable as long as he gave his patrons the rest of the museum's attractions for their admission fee. Even though Barnum maintained that he carried out his hoaxes to generate business for his museum, he has been criticized for being dishonest. Yet, Barnum always enjoyed a good joke. His so-called frauds may well have been practical jokes on the public. There is much evidence that people accepted them as such.

When Barnum sponsored his "Great Buffalo Hunt" a few years later, the public probably enjoyed the spectacle as much as he did. At that time, thousands of buffalo were still running free on the western plains of the United States, since this area had not yet been settled. New Yorkers had heard of buffalo, but few had ever seen one, let alone a buffalo hunt. Barnum was well aware of this when he bought a herd of fifteen yearling buffalo for seven hundred dollars. He stabled them in a New Jersey barn and hired their former owner, C.D. French, as caretaker. Then, as he had done with the Fejee Mermaid, he kept his name out of it while he built up public interest with a series of letters to the newspapers. Before long, advertisements for the "Great Buffalo Hunt" appeared throughout New York. Handbills and posters announced that the hunt was to be held at a racetrack in Hoboken, New Jersey—free of charge! C.D. French was billed as "one of the most daring and experienced hunters of the West," who would demonstrate his skill in hunting and with the lasso. People were assured that they would be protected from the ferocious wild beasts by a double-railing fence.

When the day for the hunt came, the poor calves were still tired after their long journey from the western plains. Although Barnum had fed them well, they had not recovered from the thin rations they had received while under French's ownership. They stood huddled together, more frightened than ferocious. They refused to move no matter what French, dressed as an American Indian, did. After a few minutes of this, the spectators broke into deafening laughter. The startled buffalo began to trot. The crowd cheered. Crashing through the double fence, the buffalo galloped to a nearby swamp. French chased after them, but nothing he could do would get them to return to the racetrack. He finally lassoed one unfortunate buffalo and dragged it back. Then he entertained the crowd with an exhibition of lassoing. It was not much of a show, but few, if any, of the spectators complained.

On the contrary, when people just arriving for the next performance of the "Great Buffalo Hunt" asked those leaving about it, they were told it was the biggest humbug that they had ever heard of. The incoming crowd gave three cheers for the author of the humbug, whoever he might be. After all, the show was free and so was the music. The only cost had been twelve-and-a-half cents for the round-trip fare from New York.

And how had Barnum profited? He had chartered all the Hudson River ferryboats and had rented out refreshment stands, so he pocketed all the profits made that day. And after the hunt was over, he sold some of the herd in England, while the rest became buffalo steak at fifty cents a pound.

After the public enjoyed a laugh for several days, Barnum announced that he was responsible for the joke. He had used the buffalo hunt as a skyrocket to attract public attention to his American Museum. As time went on and Barnum became more and more successful, he depended less and less on humbuggery. Although he no longer needed hoaxes to publicize his museum, he still carried them out for his own amusement.

Barnum pulled several publicity stunts like the "Great Buffalo Hunt" scheme and pioneered many methods used by press agents and publicity seekers today. He spent hours dreaming up newsworthy actions that would receive a line or two in the papers. Once, Barnum tried to buy the cottage at Stratford-on-Avon, England, where William Shakespeare was born in 1564. He planned to ship it from England in sections and put it together again inside the American Museum. At the time, the neglected house had a butcher shop in its living room. When Barnum made

his offer, however, the people of England were out-
raged. A few wealthy Londoners got together and
bought the cottage to prevent Barnum from taking it.
Eventually, the cottage was restored and dedicated as
a national monument, and today, thousands of tour-
ists visit it every year.

In 1858, the first communication cable was laid
across the Atlantic Ocean. Barnum offered five thousand dollars for the privilege of sending the first
twenty-word message between England and the
United States over the new cable. His offer was refused and Queen Victoria sent a message to President
James Buchanan instead. Barnum did not really expect his offer to be accepted, but he thought that if
he had gotten the chance to send across the first
words, the publicity would have been worth a million
dollars to him.

Over the years, Barnum worked continually to
make sure that the American Museum was well
stocked. He expanded the museum with thousands of
permanent legitimate attractions. In addition, he
bought or hired curiosities to display for a short time.
He exhibited rhinoceros, giraffes, grizzly bears, oran-
gutans, great serpents, and whatever else he could get.
The first hippopotamus seen by Americans was exhibited in the American Museum. Some of his most
outstanding human attractions were Madame Cloful-
lia, the original Bearded Lady; Young Herman, the
expansionist who could inflate his chest from thirty-

eight to sixty inches; Anna Swan, a giantess who was seven feet eleven inches tall and weighed over four hundred pounds; Captain Bates, a giant who married Anna Swan; other giants and several midgets; and Chang and Eng, the original Siamese twins. Barnum gave the English language this new phrase when he introduced Chang and Eng to the world. They were not the first pair of babies born with their bodies joined together. But they were the first to receive wide publicity.

Chang and Eng were born in 1811 to poor Chinese parents who were living in Siam (now Thailand). When they were nineteen, they were found by a Captain Coffin, who ran a Yankee schooner between the United States and China. He put them under contract and exhibited them in England and Europe as the "Siamese Double Boys." After they arrived in the United States, Barnum bought their contract from Captain Coffin. The "Siamese Double Boys" did not sound right to Barnum's ear, so he changed their title to the "Siamese Twins."

Although they were bound together for life at the base of their rib cages, they disliked each other and often quarreled. Once they came to blows and ended up in court. No doubt one reason they argued was that they were very different in many ways. Eng was cheerful and outgoing. Chang was often moody and irritable. What Chang liked to eat, Eng hated. When one was ill, the other was usually in good health. Their

Chang and Eng, the original Siamese twins, were star attractions for years at P.T. Barnum's American Museum.

only common interests were fishing, hunting, and wood-cutting. In spite of their difficulties, the Siamese Twins were museum favorites for years and retired as wealthy men. And ever since, all connected twins are referred to as Siamese.

Besides expanding and improving the exhibits, Barnum converted the small lecture room into a large and beautiful theater, which could hold up to three thousand people. At first, the lecture room was open only in the evenings, but soon it filled for afternoon shows as well. On holidays, Barnum often had as many as twelve performances.

Barnum constantly changed the attractions offered in the lecture room. One week, he might feature educated dogs, a flea circus, jugglers, and a ventriloquist. Another week he would present gypsies, a fat boy, a giant or two, several dwarfs, and a troupe of ropedancers. Pantomimes, singers and dancers, fancy glassblowers, the first English puppet show of Punch and Judy in this country, and American Indians who performed their war and religious ceremonies—all, in turn, were hired to entertain Barnum's patrons.

Ever conscious of the general public's condemnation of entertainment, Barnum would not let his lecture room be called a theater, and at first he presented his attractions as educational features. Gradually, he introduced plays which were considered moral or educational. They often had religious themes, and of course all vulgar language was removed. Barnum made a point of inviting women and children to see his plays, assuring them that they would find nothing upsetting in them. He was so successful in disguising his plays that most people did not think they were actually attending the theater.

Chapter Six

General Tom Thumb

Barnum made one of the most remarkable discoveries of his career because a river froze over. In November of 1842, near the end of his first year at the American Museum, Barnum visited Albany, New York, on museum business. He had planned to return home by taking a boat down the Hudson River to New York City, but found he could not because the water was frozen. He ended up taking a train instead.

Since the train passed through Bridgeport, Connecticut, where his half-brother, Philo, managed the Franklin Hotel, Barnum decided to stay there overnight. After Philo told Barnum about Charles Stratton, a midget he had seen playing in the streets of Bridgeport, Barnum made arrangements to meet the boy and his parents. And when he saw Charles Stratton the next day, Barnum knew at once he could make the boy into a star attraction.

Charles Stratton was the smallest child Barnum had ever seen who could walk alone. He was a perfectly proportioned five-year-old child with pale blond hair, sparkling dark eyes, and ruddy cheeks. Yet, he was only twenty-three inches tall and weighed just fifteen pounds. His foot was three inches long, and his hand was the size of a fifty-cent piece. He was very shy but extremely intelligent.

Because doctors had not yet discovered how growth was regulated by the pituitary gland, there were hundreds of midgets at the time. Charles Stratton had the good fortune of capturing the imagination of P.T. Barnum, master showman. Barnum soon had Charles and his parents under contract, thus forming one of the most successful partnerships in the history of show business.

Barnum began Charles's education at once. He taught the boy how to speak politely, shake hands, and bow. Young Charles was eager to learn. His sharp wit and good sense of humor gave him a natural talent for performing, and he quickly learned a few stage roles to fit the costumes Barnum had ordered for him. Anxious to see if the public would be as enthusiastic as he was, Barnum had his young pupil ready for his first appearance in a week's time.

At the same time that Barnum was coaching Charles, he was starting his advertising campaign to alert the public to his newest attraction. He knew that a five-year-old midget from a nearby town with the ordinary-sounding name of Charles Stratton might not cause much excitement. So, just as he had done with Signor Vivalla, the plate-juggling stilt walker, Barnum made some changes. First, there was the matter of age. An eleven-year-old under two feet tall would be much more impressive than a five-year-old the same size, he decided. Then, knowing that the American public favored foreign entertainers, Barnum decided that Charles should be billed as an Englishman.

And finally, Barnum wanted to find an unusual name for his pupil. Inspiration struck when he remembered that most people knew the story of Tom Thumb. This legendary inch-tall knight lived at King Arthur's court in a tiny gold palace and rode a carriage pulled by six white mice. After many adventures, he was killed by a bee. Barnum thought that "Tom Thumb" was the perfect stage name for young Charles. Adding the title of "General" was a stroke of genius. There was a magical quality to the name "General Tom Thumb" that grabbed the public's imagination.

Soon Barnum had flooded New York with advertisements and billboards. In them, five-year-old Charles Stratton of Bridgeport became "General Tom Thumb, the celebrated dwarf of eleven, just arrived from England." (Barnum was mistaken in referring to his pupil as a dwarf. Charles Stratton was a midget—a perfectly proportioned, small human being. A dwarf

P.T. Barnum stands side by side with General Tom Thumb, who entertained audiences from the American Museum in New York to the court of Queen Victoria in London.

has a body that is out of proportion in some way.)

Before putting General Tom Thumb on stage, Barnum took him to meet various newspaper reporters in order to generate some free publicity. In one instance he interrupted an editor's dinner. General Tom Thumb was lifted to the tabletop where he marched back and forth, pushing aside dishes and glasses with his foot and entertaining the editor's guests with clever remarks. He captured the hearts of all he met and Barnum was rewarded with a flood of favorable "printer's ink."

A full house crowded the lecture room for Tom Thumb's first performance. Dressed in the uniform of a Continental soldier with a white wig and a cocked hat, he opened with a monologue filled with puns written by Barnum. "I'm only a Thumb, but a good hand at amusing you! I may be a mite, but I'm mighty! Though I grow in your favor, no taller I'd be! I'm great while I'm small so I don't want to rise!" he exclaimed. Then he had a humorous dialogue with Barnum concerning his background and his size. Next, he performed a military drill—marching, saluting, and brandishing his ten-inch sword at the audience. For a finish, he strutted about singing "Yankee-Doodle" and trotted off the stage. In later performances, he danced the polka, the sailor's hornpipe, and the highland fling.

Tom Thumb was a hit from his first appearance. Because museum business took up most of Barnum's

time, he hired a friend to tutor his star. Besides teaching the general, the tutor traveled with Tom Thumb
and his parents. He acted as a sort of bodyguard to
them, keeping away jealous showmen who might try
to hire the general away from Barnum.

With his tutor's help, Tom Thumb learned a
series of short skits in which he acted like various
people from history and legend, among them Napoleon, Frederick the Great, Hercules, Samson, and a
Fighting Gladiator. As the biblical David, he fought
one of the museum's giants, who was dressed as Go-
liath. Equipped with gauzy wings and flesh-colored
tights, he imitated Cupid and skipped around the
stage firing pencil-sized arrows across the footlights
with his miniature bow. Women battled to catch the
arrows as souvenirs, showered him with gifts, bought
his photograph, begged for his tiny autograph, and
blew him kisses. Seeing Tom Thumb became the fa-
shionable thing to do. After he had conquered New
York, the little general, in the care of one of Barnum's
trusted assistants, toured the rest of the country with
equal success, making money for Barnum and himself.

In January of 1844, Barnum decided to take Tom
Thumb to Europe. His museum, bought in 1842, was
paid for, and he felt it would be safe to leave it for his
associates to run. He had money in the bank, and he
was restless. He needed a new challenge. Outside of
the United States, Barnum was unknown. "Invading"
England so soon after the Revolutionary War to

launch General Tom Thumb was a daring move that excited the Yankee showman.

Barnum, Tom Thumb, his mother and father, his tutor, and several of Barnum's friends set sail for England on January 18, 1844. Ten thousand people and a municipal brass band stood by the dock to see them off. When they arrived at Liverpool, England, they were greeted by crowds eager to see General Tom Thumb. His fame had already spread across the Atlantic. To protect her son from possible injury from overenthusiastic crowds, Mrs. Stratton carried him ashore in her arms like a baby.

One of General Tom Thumb's early appearances was at the court of Queen Victoria. There, he and Barnum were received in the picture gallery by the queen, her husband Prince Albert, and other members of royalty. The queen took the little general by the hand, led him through the gallery, and asked him many questions. His witty answers kept his royal audience laughing almost constantly. The general then performed his songs, dances, and imitations. Afterwards, he talked with Prince Albert and the other people present, while Barnum told Queen Victoria about Tom Thumb's background. Their visit lasted almost an hour. Queen Victoria must have been truly enchanted with her small guest because such a long audience with a queen was unusual.

Before the audience with the queen, Barnum and Tom Thumb had been told the proper way to leave the room. When it was time to go, they remembered their instructions. The pair started to back out of the one-hundred-fifty-foot gallery, always keeping their faces toward the queen. The little general did his best, but he could not keep pace with Barnum. Whenever he saw that Barnum was too far ahead of him, he turned and ran a few steps. Then turning back toward the queen again, he bowed and continued his walk backwards. He continued in this manner, walking backwards and then running forward until everyone in the royal audience was laughing.

Barnum and Tom Thumb visited Queen Victoria three times and after each visit, they received a large payment in gold. These audiences with Queen Victoria excited the British public. The people loved their queen and usually followed the examples she set. What Queen Victoria enjoyed, everyone in London was prepared to enjoy, so when Tom Thumb began giving public performances, his shows were continually crowded with people eager to see the famous general.

He performed daily at Egyptian Hall in London and made private appearances in the homes of the English nobility, for which Barnum charged fifty dollars. The general also appeared at orphanages without charge. Pictures of him were everywhere. Songs were sung in his honor in the London amusement halls; music was dedicated to him; and polka and quadrille dances were named after him. Albert

Smith wrote a special play for him called *Hop o' My Thumb*, which the general performed at the Lyceum Theatre. Children even played with Tom Thumb paper dolls.

After winning London's favor, General Tom Thumb toured the rest of England with great success. Then Barnum took him to Paris, where he became even more popular than he had been in England. Plaster, sugar, and chocolate statues of *Le Général Tom Pouce* appeared in the shop windows. A restaurant was named after him and displayed his life-sized figure over its door. Tom Thumb had three meetings with the French king, Louis-Philippe, and even received a special invitation to the king's birthday party.

After a three-month engagement in Paris, Tom Thumb toured throughout France, appearing nightly in a play after being on exhibit during the day. From France, Barnum took Tom Thumb to Spain, Belgium, Scotland, Ireland, and again to England.

During the three years that Barnum stayed with Tom Thumb in Europe, he went back to the United States twice to visit his family and to check on his museum. He also brought his family to England for an extended stay. When he was not supervising Tom Thumb's appearances, he was busy writing articles for the New York papers and gathering more curiosities for his museum.

Barnum returned to the United States in 1847 a very rich man. As for Tom Thumb, in those three

years abroad he had become equal partners with
Barnum and was a very rich nine-year-old boy, having earned over seven hundred thousand dollars. Besides, he had learned to speak French and Spanish, he
played the piano and violin, and he was a clever con-
versationalist. He still weighed fifteen pounds, but he
was now twenty-five inches tall.

Barnum and Tom Thumb would work together as
partners for the next thirty years, with Barnum providing someone to travel with the Tom Thumb company as general manager and advance publicity man.
Eventually, the general owned a country estate outside Bridgeport, a stable of horses, and a large yacht,
which he sailed on Long Island Sound.

In 1862 Tom Thumb was twenty-four and had
grown to thirty-three inches in height. He weighed
fifty pounds. Between tours he met Lavinia Warren, a
thirty-two-inch midget and a third grade teacher who
had become the star of Barnum's museum show. It
was love at first sight. They were married on February
10, 1863, in New York's Grace Church. On their
wedding trip, they visited Abraham Lincoln at the
White House. Lincoln asked the general if he had any
suggestions about how to conduct the Civil War that
was raging at the time. Tom Thumb replied, "Mr.
President, my friend Barnum could settle the whole
thing in a month."

Some reports say that one child, a girl, was born
of the marriage. Supposedly, she only lived two-and-

*On the day of their wedding, Tom Thumb (1838-1883) stands beside
his bride, Lavinia Warren (1841-1919). Their real names were Charles
Sherwood Stratton and Lavinia Warren Bumpus.*

Mr. & Mrs. "General Tom Thumb"
in their wedding costume.

a-half years, dying of what was diagnosed as "inflammation of the brain." Other accounts say that the child never lived—that rumors of her existence were just another publicity stunt on Barnum's part. Today, the actual facts are still uncertain.

Tom Thumb and Lavinia had intended to retire to his estate in Bridgeport, but they loved show business too much to stay away long. They started to perform again. Together they made a number of exhibition tours in the United States and Europe until Tom Thumb's death in 1883, at the age of forty-five.

Chapter/Seven

I risked much, but I gained more

When Barnum retired from active management of Tom Thumb in May of 1848, he settled with his family in Bridgeport, Connecticut, where builders had just finished Iranistan, the first of his four homes. At first Barnum enjoyed a semi-retired life, traveling to New York a day or so a week to attend to the American Museum and other business interests. He was a wealthy man, known nationwide as the world's greatest showman. Yet, he was not satisfied. He wanted to be known as a friend and sponsor of artists instead of just an exhibitor of curiosities.

At that time, music was not flourishing in the United States. No outstanding homegrown artists had been developed, and singers who could still please European audiences did not consider a trip to the "colonies" worthwhile. They either visited there before they were famous or at the end of their careers.

These facts did not stop Barnum. He believed that he would improve his social standing and gain new friends if he brought to the United States Jenny Lind, who was captivating audiences all over Europe. Yet she was almost unknown to Americans. Indeed, Barnum had never seen her or heard her sing. But he felt that if he brought the greatest wonder of the world to America, he would be recognized as a man of culture. Of course, he also thought he had an excellent chance of making money.

Jenny Lind, known as the Swedish Nightingale, was born in Stockholm, Sweden, in 1820. When she was only three years old, she could pick out a tune on a piano. She was about ten when she received a contract from the Stockholm Royal Theater, where she began as an actress. At seventeen, she began to sing professionally in operas. Because of her strict religious upbringing, Jenny Lind found it difficult, since operas are often based on highly emotional and passionate stories. She did it only because she felt it was the quickest way for her to accomplish her greatest dream: to give a hospital to Stockholm for its poor children. By the spring of 1849, her objections to the stage had grown so intense that she decided to retire from the opera. However, she had not reached the goal she had set for her hospital fund-raising because she had been so generous to other charities.

Soon after Jenny Lind's retirement, Barnum sent his agent to see her. In January, 1850, she signed a contract to sing in the United States at one hundred and fifty concerts under Barnum's management. She did not need the money for herself, but she welcomed the chance to earn the rest of the money for her hospital without ever again having to sing on the operatic stage.

In the contract, Barnum agreed to pay Jenny Lind one thousand dollars for each performance; furnish her with a maid, a butler, and a secretary; and pay all expenses for her and her staff, including a companion to keep her company and to take care of little problems that might occur. Barnum also agreed to pay all the expenses for Julius Benedict, her musical director, and for Giovanni Belletti, a baritone who would also appear on her program. Jenny Lind would not sail from Europe, however, until Barnum placed $187,000 with his London bankers as a guarantee.

Although Barnum was a wealthy man, raising $187,000 in cash presented a challenge. When he gathered together his available funds, he found he was considerably short. He tried to get a loan from the bank where he had done business for eight years, but the president of the bank laughed in his face, saying, "Mr. Barnum, it is generally believed on Wall Street that your engagement with Jenny Lind will ruin you." Barnum was not discouraged by the banker's reply. He sold several pieces of property for cash and accepted a loan of $5,000 from a friend. In late winter of 1850, the $187,000 was finally deposited with his

Jenny Lind, known as the Swedish Nightingale, became an overnight sensation in the United States when she went on a concert tour arranged by P.T. Barnum.

London bank, and Jenny Lind agreed to sail for America in the fall.

There was another obstacle to overcome, however. Although Jenny Lind was famous throughout Europe, most Americans had never heard of her. Barnum knew he had a tremendous selling job to do and only seven months to accomplish it before Jenny Lind's opening performance in September. He knew he would have to work hard if he was to make back his $187,000 advance, let alone make a profit. He began to prepare the public for Jenny Lind's arrival in the United States, once again relying on the newspapers. First, he wrote a letter that appeared in the New York papers on February 23, 1850. In it, he described Jenny Lind's gifts to charity, which were considerable, and only once mentioned her singing ability. In later promotions, he continued to emphasize her desire to raise money for charity because he knew the American public would attend her performances, regardless of how she sang, lured by her generosity to others.

From then on, Barnum used every method he could think of to get Jenny Lind's name and reputation before the public. He hired a reporter to write two or three columns a week, supposedly from London, about Jenny's popularity and charitable activities. Soon publishers began to circulate biographies of her. Then, inspired by Barnum's publicity, Jenny Lind songbooks, gloves, hats, shawls, dolls, robes, chairs, sofas, pianos, and many other items were sold everywhere. (The Jenny Lind bed is still a popular item in the antique market today.) Her picture was displayed throughout the country. A merchant ship, a brand of whiskey, and a racehorse were all christened "Jenny Lind." Barnum was overwhelmingly successful in his efforts to make Jenny Lind's name a household word.

By the time the Swedish Nightingale arrived in New York on September 1, 1850, all America was eager to see her. A crowd of thirty thousand welcomed her boat as it docked. As the ship's captain escorted her down the gangplank, Barnum employees showered her with huge bouquets. Five thousand people greeted her when she arrived at her hotel, and within ten minutes, the crowd had swelled to twenty thousand. People stayed on for six hours, cheering and calling for a glimpse of the singer.

The excitement continued for the next ten days before Jenny's first concert on September 11 at the Castle Garden, the largest amusement hall in the city of New York. Barnum auctioned off tickets for the first concert and the first buyer paid $225 for the privilege of hearing Jenny Lind's first American concert. Some bidders paid as little as $3. The five thousand people who attended the opening night cheered, screamed, threw hats and handkerchiefs, and screamed some more when the Swedish Nightingale first appeared on the stage. And after the concert, the whole scene was repeated when Barnum announced that Jenny Lind was donating her entire share of the profits to various New York charities.

Jenny Lind gave six concerts in New York before going on to Boston. Here Barnum again auctioned the tickets to the first concert. The first ticket sold for $625. After Boston, Jenny Lind sang in dozens of cities in the eastern states. Midway through the tour, the group spent a month in Havana, Cuba, where Jenny Lind gave four concerts.

The stay in Havana was a pleasant one, but other times were less pleasant. In large part this was due to the people in the singer's company. Barnum felt that some of them were selfish, greedy hangers-on. The male secretary, whom Jenny Lind had brought with her from Europe, wanted to take over as her business manager and share in the profits. He constantly tried to turn her against Barnum, saying, among other things, that he was growing rich on her talent and that Barnum's publicity was more fitting for a circus than for the Swedish Nightingale. Others in the group quit and returned to Europe over the course of the tour.

To add to Barnum's problems, he discovered that his singer was temperamental. He made sure no hint of her outbursts and tantrums ever reached the public ear. It was simply his policy to present her as being charming and gracious, no matter how it made him appear. The newspapers often carried stories that praised Jenny Lind's donations to charity. However, they criticized Barnum for not being as generous. For several weeks in October of 1850, James Gorden

Bennet attacked Barnum in his newspaper, the *Herald*. He wanted to know when Barnum would follow Jenny Lind's example. "[Barnum] has not given a penny as yet for any charitable purpose," he wrote, "although he makes more out of Jenny's talents than Jenny herself does."

While it was true that Jenny Lind donated her voice when she gave a concert for charity, it was Barnum who paid the costs of the hall, the orchestra, the printing, and the advertising from his own pocket. Although he contributed largely to his singer's charities, he did not take credit for it, partly because it was his nature not to expect praise for his actions. He also knew that the success of the tour depended upon the public's seeing Jenny Lind as the most angelic and charitable of women. He did not want to do or say anything that would spoil that image.

Tensions grew. The agreed-upon concerts to be held under Barnum's management dropped from one hundred and fifty to one hundred. Then, in early June of 1851, the two agreed to part company after the ninety-third concert. At that point, the gross receipts for the concerts totaled just over $680,000. Of that, Jenny realized almost $177,000 after expenses and Barnum made approximately $215,000. His profits would have been greater if he had not decided to pay her twice as much as her original contract required.

After leaving Barnum's management, Jenny Lind gave several concerts, but they were only moderately successful. What she had not realized was that the crowds that flocked to her concerts under Barnum's management had not been gathered by her musical genius alone. Barnum's promotion was the key to her success, even if her secretary characterized the publicity as fit only for a circus.

On May 24, 1852, Jenny Lind gave a farewell American concert at Castle Garden. When she sailed for England, only two thousand people saw her off since there was no Barnum to dramatize her departure. Jenny Lind settled in England, where she abandoned her career except to sing for every needy cause that attracted her attention.

As for Barnum, he was happy that the ninemonth tour was over. He said that he had not known a waking moment that was entirely free from anxiety. It had been worth all the effort and worry, however. "It placed me before the world in a new light," Barnum said. "It gained for me many warm friends in new circles. . .I risked much, but I gained more."

Jenny Lind's tour marked the beginning of real music in the United States. It set the fashion of importing famous singers to America while they were in the prime of their careers. Indirectly, it led to the foundation of the Metropolitan Opera Company of New York. And perhaps more important, Americans with musical talent were encouraged to develop it. Gradually, musical concerts became accepted as an important part of American life.

Chapter/Eight

The art of money getting—and losing

Although Barnum had boundless energy, he was exhausted at the end of his tour with Jenny Lind. Keeping his star and her company happy had been an endless, and often thankless, job. When he gave up his job as Jenny Lind's manager in 1851, he felt he needed peace and quiet. He spent a week of vacation at Cape May in New Jersey, and then returned home to Iranistan on Long Island Sound in Bridgeport, Connecticut.

Iranistan had been constructed while he was touring Europe with Tom Thumb. In England, Barnum had visited a royal pavilion, one of the first English examples of oriental-style architecture, and he had been favorably impressed. He arranged for the building of an American version while he was still abroad. It took workers two full years to build the main house. When they finished, it was over a hundred feet across the front and three stories high. A central onion-shaped dome reached nearly a hundred feet into the air, and surrounding it were spires, turrets, and minarets. Domed greenhouses bulged at either end.

Inside, the great hallway and wide, winding, marble staircase were lined with pictures, statues, and other works of art from all over the world. Barnum ordered special furniture made for each room, some carved with snakes, birds, and other creatures.

A seventeen-acre park enclosed by an iron fence surrounded the house. Fountains were scattered about the grounds and full-grown trees, which had been transplanted from forests, provided shade. A stable and several barns filled with livestock also occupied the park. The New York and New Haven Railroad ran nearby, so besides building a home, Barnum had erected an eye-catching group of buildings that he felt indirectly advertised his museum to the train passengers.

From the latter part of 1851 to 1855, he stayed at Iranistan, living in semi-retirement. This was the longest, uninterrupted period that Barnum had ever lived with his family since his marriage to Charity in 1829. Because Barnum spent most of his years in public life, very little is known of his private personality and even less is known of his private life.

During this time, he wrote his autobiography, *The Life of P. T. Barnum, Written by Himself,* which he

P.T. Barnum goes for a ride in his carriage. At Iranistan Barnum worked in the morning and spent time with his family and friends in the afternoon and evening.

revised, enlarged, and reissued seven times before he died. In this book, Barnum describes some of the details of day-to-day life at Iranistan. Barnum says he was moderate in his habits. When at home, he followed a rigid routine, rising at seven in the morning, and going to bed at ten in the evening. He spent the mornings at his desk writing and answering letters or conducting business affairs. He usually worked until about noon. Then after a ride in his carriage, he had a large midday meal with his family. In the evenings Barnum read or had a few friends or neighbors over to play cards, but they were expected to leave by nine-thirty. And Barnum reminded them if they forgot!

Barnum was proud of his wine cellar at Iranistan and consumed an entire bottle of champagne at lunch every day. Charity spent many nights crying herself to sleep because she feared he was on the path toward alcoholism. But she said nothing, knowing her warnings would only make her husband angry. One day Barnum heard a temperance lecture by his friend, the Reverend E.H. Chapin, who preached against the drinking of all alcoholic beverages. As a result, Barnum was completely convinced that his wine-drinking could turn him into a drunkard. He went home, poured out all his champagne, and signed a teetotal pledge in which he promised never again to drink any kind of alcoholic beverage. When he told Charity what he had done, she wept for joy.

The day he signed the pledge, he decided it was his duty to set out at once to preach temperance, urging everyone he met to stop drinking beer, wine, and whiskey. He talked twenty friends into signing the pledge that day. Soon he was giving lectures to various groups on the evils of drinking. During late 1851 and early 1852, he traveled the entire state of Connecticut at his own expense to deliver free talks on the subject.

Barnum smoked ten cigars a day. He found it more difficult to conquer this habit. He tried to stop several times, but without success. Then one day in 1860 when he was fifty, he had a fit of coughing. His heart began to beat so fast that he was sure he was dying of a heart attack. He hurried to his doctor, who assured him that his heart was fine. It was the nicotine from the cigars that was causing his problem. "Stop smoking," his doctor advised him. And Barnum did, this time for good.

Except for an occasional game of billiards, he disliked athletics. Barnum played cards, but was a poor loser and often embarrassed his guests with his lack of sportsmanship. He found that practicing ventriloquism, performing card tricks, and imitating the many celebrities he knew were activities he liked better.

Barnum enjoyed reading, however, and was quite a letter writer. From his youth to his old age, he wrote letter after letter to the editors of newspapers. It was his favorite way to get his ideas before the public. He often got up at four in the morning and wrote for hours. When he wished to criticize a member of his family, he often left a note where he was sure it would be found. And, when Barnum traveled, he sent letters back to his family twice a week.

On these trips, if he were close enough to home, he tried to spend Sundays with his family. Although Barnum still attended church regularly with his wife, he had, like his Grandfather Taylor before him, turned away from the strict Puritan beliefs of his youth. And like his Grandfather Taylor, he joined the Universalist church, whose members believed that their God was a God of love who would not punish wrongdoers with hell. In the end, everyone would be saved and enter heaven. Barnum also developed a firm faith that the God he believed in would always take care of him. Because of this belief, he seldom worried, and was almost always cheerful no matter what happened to him.

Very little is known about Barnum's wife Charity and their daughters Caroline, Helen, Frances, and Pauline, who had been born in 1846. Frances died in infancy. Barnum was constantly in the headlines, but he somehow managed to keep his family affairs out of the newspapers. And in the several versions of his autobiography, he does not often mention Charity or his daughters.

It is known that Charity was never physically strong, and that her health slowly declined after their four children were born. Her role as the wife of such a public man must have been difficult and lonely because she was a homebody who liked nothing better than to putter with her flowers in the greenhouses. One of her few interests outside her home was the Bridgeport Charitable Society. Barnum often asked her to accompany him on trips, but she refused his invitations except for making two trips to London with the children. Barnum seldom discussed personal affairs with her. Although people remembered him as a thoughtful and kind man, he did not tell Charity when, for a time, he was seriously considering selling

Iranistan and moving to Philadelphia. He left it to their oldest daughter Caroline to break the news to her mother. He later reconsidered, and the family remained at Iranistan.

Barnum enjoyed his children's companionship when he was at home and admitted that he spoiled them with almost unlimited spending money. Barnum loved his family and home, but like some other successful people, he did not have very much time to devote to them. Nor did he have much time to think or talk about them.

Success came to Barnum because of many things, among them his ability to keep trying despite all difficulties and his ability to adjust to the many changes that occurred during his lifetime. He was, for example, one of the first people in the country to install a telephone in his home.

Barnum thoroughly enjoyed his world, his work, and himself. Probably the one characteristic that dominated in Barnum's personality was his unlimited optimism. He wrote that his personality caused him to look upon the brighter side of life. And Barnum's ability to look upon the brighter side of life was put to the test by the events of the next few years.

During this time Barnum kept careful control of the American Museum, although he only visited New York once or twice a week. He conducted museum business at home, always working to make its collection larger and better. In 1855, feeling he was wealthy enough to retire from active business, he sold the contents of the American Museum. He kept title to the building, however, in his wife's name. Soon, though, he became restless under the leisurely life he was living. He was only forty-one and bursting with energy.

Always on the lookout for new adventures, he soon involved himself in the affairs of Bridgeport and the surrounding areas. He became the president of the Pequonnock Bank of Bridgeport and was elected president of the Fairfield County Agricultural Society.

Barnum's biggest project was the creation of a new city. In 1851 he joined William Noble in building an industrial community on 224 acres of land across the Pequonnock River from Bridgeport. In a few years, the city, called East Bridgeport, was flourishing with churches, a school, and a horse railway. A carriage maker, sewing machine factory, and other industries hired thousands of employees.

It seemed as if the project was a tremendous success. Then came Barnum's downfall. He was not wise in most matters outside of show business, and his good sense was overcome by his ambitions for East Bridgeport.

In 1855 the owners of the Jerome Clock Company approached him with a proposition. They would move their factory from New Haven, Connecticut, to East Bridgeport in return for financial assistance in clearing up their debts.

A new factory would bring workers and their families to East Bridgeport, Barnum reasoned. The city would grow and the value of the property would increase. Because he was eager to help his new city, he accepted the plan.

What followed was a series of complicated financial maneuvers by the Jerome Clock Company. At the end of three months, Barnum was stunned to discover that he had spent five hundred thousand dollars paying off the clock company's debts. Worse yet, both he and the Jerome Clock Company were bankrupt. And to top off the whole disaster, the clock company never did move to East Bridgeport although this had been the only reason that Barnum had agreed to lend the money to it in the first place.

At forty-five years of age, Barnum had made and lost a fortune. Everything was gone, even his beloved Iranistan. Barnum had moved his family to rented quarters in New York City in the early part of 1857. He had hoped eventually to buy back his home, but it burned to the ground in December of that year. The family did not have to live in poverty, however. Barnum had given the American Museum building to his wife several years before, and Charity received nineteen thousand dollars a year rent from it. With this, she was able to meet their daily needs and help pay off Barnum's debts.

As a result of his financial troubles, Barnum now received a different kind of treatment. Those who had fawned over him when he was on top of the world jeered him when he was on the bottom. Newspapers editorialized that this was the end of Barnum's life as a successful showman.

But Barnum had his supporters, too. They offered not only sympathy for his problems, but also money to support his family and reestablish him in business. He refused all offers, however. He was sure that with hard work and the help of his God, he would get back on his feet again. "The situation," he said, "was disheartening, but I had energy, experience, health, and hope."

Early in 1857, Barnum felt he needed a change of scenery. Leaving his business affairs in the hands of friends, he set sail for England, taking with him Tom Thumb and the Howard family, which had just finished a successful four-year tour of the United States with the play, *Uncle Tom's Cabin*. He was determined to make as much money as he could with these two attractions.

General Tom Thumb, returning after so long an absence, drew crowds wherever he went in London and the provinces of England, and in France, the Netherlands, and Germany. The Howards' production of *Uncle Tom's Cabin* was a great success in London. Barnum was able to send thousands of dollars home to help dig himself out of debt.

In time, Barnum turned over the day-to-day management of Tom Thumb's tour to his agents. Then he

looked for something else to do, always aware of the
fact that he had to use every possible opportunity to
make money. Some friends suggested that he give a
lecture on "*The Art of Money Getting.*" Barnum replied that considering his dark misfortunes he might
speak better on "*The Art of Money Losing.*"

His friends reminded him that he had to have the
ability to make money before he could lose it. And
finally, Barnum accepted their suggestion. Three thousand people attended the first lecture, given on December 29, 1858. During 1859 he delivered this speech
nearly one hundred times in different parts of England, returning to London occasionally to repeat it to
new audiences. His efforts earned him a substantial
sum of money to use toward paying off his debt and
Barnum made many new friends on his journey.

By March of 1860, five years after his bank-
ruptcy, Barnum was able to pay off all his debts and
buy back the collection in the American Museum.

He was not quite fifty years old.

Chapter/Nine

Time hung on my hands

From 1860 to 1865, Barnum was back doing what he liked to do and what seemed best suited to his talents. These were the years of his greatest success with the museum. Once again, he sent his agents to the far corners of the world in search of curiosities for display. During this time, he laid a system of iron pipes under the city streets, from his museum to the ocean waters of New York Bay. Through it he piped salt water into a special tank on the second floor of the museum. Thousands of people flocked there to get their first look at live white whales, sharks, sea horses, and rare tropical fish.

In 1861 Barnum signed a three-year contract with George Washington Morrison Nutt, who was to be among his dozen greatest attractions of all time. Handsome and cocky, Nutt was eighteen years old, twenty-nine inches tall, and weighed twenty-four pounds.

Barnum agreed to pay him ten thousand dollars a year plus expenses for himself and a companion. As he had done before, he soon found a way to make his newest attraction distinctive. Barnum gave him the title of "Commodore." Then he furnished him with a naval uniform and a carriage patterned after an English walnut shell, which was pulled by ponies in gold-mounted harnesses.

In 1862 Barnum took Commodore Nutt to the White House to meet President Lincoln. As they were leaving, Lincoln bent his long, lean body to shake the midget's little hand and said, "Commodore, permit me to give you a parting word of advice. When you are in command of your fleet, if you find yourself in danger of being taken prisoner, I'd advise you to wade ashore."

Nutt placed himself beside the president, and gradually raised his eyes up the whole length of Lincoln's long legs. "I guess, Mr. President," he said, "you could do that better than I could."

The commodore lost the great love of his life, Lavinia Warren, when she married General Tom Thumb in 1863. He often toured with the general and his wife, however. And in 1872 he joined them and Lavinia Thumb's sister Minnie Warren, on a world tour, visiting Australia, China, and Japan, as well as several European countries. Commodore Nutt died several years later in 1881. He was thirty-three and still a bachelor.

Besides obtaining new displays for his museum, Barnum looked for attractions to sponsor outside of it. Sometimes people looked for him, as did James C. "Grizzly" Adams.

Adams had been a part of that vast mob of people who invaded California during the gold rush of 1849. He became disgusted by the greed and corruption that he saw there and decided to try and find a new life in the western wilderness. He turned to hunting and trapping. Eventually he trapped giant grizzly bears, other species of bear, elk, buffalo, wolves, and a huge sea lion called Old Neptune. Then, he trained them as pets. He had been clawed, beaten, and almost torn limb from limb by his animals. The worst injuries were to his head, which had been bashed in many times when he was playing with his grizzlies, finally leaving a gaping wound. The doctors told him he did not have much longer to live. When he died, "Grizzly" Adams wanted to leave some money for his wife whom he had long neglected. So, he asked Barnum to sponsor a showing of his animals.

Barnum and Adams formed a partnership and exhibited the animals in a tent in New York City. On opening day, hundreds of amazed spectators watched as a brass band led a parade of the animals to the tent. Adams, mounted on a grizzly called General Frémont, rode in a wagon with three uncaged bears. Dressed in a buckskin suit trimmed with animal tails, and wearing a cap made of a wolf's head on his long, stiff, bushy,

gray hair, he almost looked like a wild creature himself. He was followed by wagons carrying cage after
cage of animals seldom seen in the eastern part of the
United States.

Although he was very weak, "Grizzly" Adams
put his animals through their acts before astonished
audiences for almost three months before he died. For
a while the grizzlies and the other animals were kept
at the museum. Later Barnum sold all but Old Neptune. Barnum considered Adams to be a real hero,
one of the most striking men of his time. His legend
has continued into the twentieth century with a tele-
vision series carrying his name.

In addition to improving the American Museum,
Barnum built a second home. Called Lindencroft (after Jenny Lind), it was placed a few hundred feet west
of where Iranistan had stood. Upon his return to
Connecticut, Barnum again became active in politics.
In 1865 he was elected to the Connecticut Assembly,
the group that made the state's laws.

On July 13, 1865, Barnum was speaking in the
Connecticut Assembly when he was handed a tele-
gram. It reported that his American Museum was in
flames, with no hope of saving any part of it. He
glanced at the note, folded it, laid it on his desk, and
continued his speech as if nothing had happened. The
museum was completely destroyed.

Barnum's first impulse was to retire from all businesses except those connected with his real estate

interests in Bridgeport. He had 150 museum employees to think about, however. Besides, Barnum felt
that New York needed a good museum and he was the
one with the experience to provide it. He rented three
adjacent buildings and quickly converted them into a
spacious museum and lecture room, filled them with
new attractions gathered by his agents, and opened
Barnum's New American Museum on November 13,
1865. Less than three years later, in March of 1868,
this museum was also destroyed by a fire which had
started in a defective chimney pipe in a restaurant on
the building's ground floor.

Before the fire, the tremendous success of his
museum had convinced Barnum that there was a need
for a great free national institution that would be
similar to the British Museum in London. He had
intended that his museum would be a part of this
institution. He also had dreams of a zoological garden for New York City. Several important people
encouraged him and signed a letter to President
Andrew Jackson in which Barnum outlined his plans.
He received the president's support, but the fire put
an end to his schemes.

This was Barnum's third fire, destroying one million dollars worth of property. It was not a great drain
on Barnum's finances, however. Part of the loss was
covered by insurance, and he had rebuilt his fortune
so that it was greater than it had been before the
Jerome Clock Company disaster. He could weather

the financial storm. Yet his great spirit of optimism
was shaken, perhaps for the first time in his life. He
took his wife, Charity, on a long vacation in the
White Mountains of northern New England while he
sorted things out. He decided to go into semi-retirement again. For a time he agreed to manage a museum
and theater for George Wood for an excellent salary.
Thus, he reasoned, he had the best of the bargain. He
could keep his hand in show business, yet not be
burdened with the problems of putting new shows
together or suffering financial headaches.

He soon found that he did not have enough to do.
He traveled with friends to Cuba and to various places
in the United States. Along the way, he stopped to
lecture on "Success in Life," "The Art of Money-get-
ting," and "Temperance." He also went on a buffalo
hunt in Kansas.

In the meantime, Charity Barnum no longer felt
able to manage Lindencroft. Her health continued to
decline, and her doctor decided that a move to the
seashore would be beneficial. Lindencroft was sold.
Barnum bought land near Seaside Park, which was
being developed under his management, and super-
vised the building of his third mansion. He called it
Waldemere, using the German words *wald* and *meer*
translated as "Woods by the Sea." The main house
and its semi-attached kitchen, the stables, the vast
lawns, the grove of trees, the walks, the shrubs and
flower beds, the statues and fountains and drives—all

were finished in less than eight months. The project required an army of workers and a great amount of money to get so much done in such a short time. When Barnum was at home, a white silk flag, with the initials PTB in blue, flew from the flagpole. Barnum enjoyed living at Waldemere and made it his home for the next twenty years.

At about the same time, Barnum bought a house in New York. He never really settled down there, although he had planned on living in it for several months during the winter. The house was used mainly for entertaining and as a base for his excursions around the country.

Even with all the traveling, lecturing, and building, Barnum still felt bored and restless. Reading did not fill enough hours even though he felt it was a pleasant enough pastime as were writing, playing chess, attending concerts and operas, and hosting dinner parties. "Time," he said, "hung on my hands."

He knew he needed a safety-valve for his pent-up energies.

Chapter/Ten

We must bring the show to you

It did not take Barnum long to find something chal-
lenging to do. In the autumn of 1870, at the age of
sixty, he began to prepare for what was to be his
greatest show of all—the circus.

Barnum did not invent circuses. The ancient Ro-
mans had a kind of circus, which consisted mainly of
horse and chariot races, and athletic contests. The
modern circus dates from the last part of the eigh-
teenth century. In fact, Barnum had visited one as a
child in the early 1800s. Circuses of that day were
held in a tent and had only one ring with a sawdust-
covered floor. There were usually six or seven boys
who did flip-flops and handsprings on horses. Besides
this act, circuses of the day included a clown who told
jokes, a magician who did a few tricks, an acrobat, or a
singer who played the banjo and danced. The circus
Barnum attended had been a simple affair, but look-

ing back years later, he said that being there gave him the happiest two hours of his life. Although circus owners had added more and more attractions throughout the years, it was Barnum who gave the circus its size, its most outstanding performers, and its widest popularity.

Although he had been a showman for years, Barnum did not have a great knowledge of the details of circus business or of its daily routine and management. He knew, however, how to assign authority to others. He had faith in his ability to choose the right people to bear the day-to-day burdens of running and promoting a circus. Once when a boy complimented him on how fine his show was, he said, "I don't know much about running a circus, but I know how to pick men who do."

Barnum took as partners W. C. Coup, an expert circus manager, and Don Costello, a famous acrobatic clown. They furnished their brains and energy. Barnum furnished the magic of his name and his money.

Called the Great Traveling World's Fair, the show opened April 20, 1871, in Brooklyn, New York, under tents that covered three acres of land. Ten thousand people filled all the available seats, and thousands more were turned away. The audience was treated to attractions that ranged from the midget, Leopold Kahn (known as "Admiral Dot"), to the eight-foot-tall Colonel Goshen (billed as the "Palestine Giant"). The two often appeared together with the admiral standing on the giant's hand. On display were Anna Leake, an armless woman; Esau, a bearded boy, and two mechanical figures, "Sleeping Beauty" and the "Dying Zouave," that seemed to breathe. Of course, clowns and jugglers also performed. And finally, there was Alexis, a circus favorite. He was an Italian goat who rode horseback. While the horse galloped at full speed, Alexis leaped through hoops and over banners, always landing on his feet on the back of the horse.

After a profitable stay in Brooklyn, Barnum and his partners successfully toured the eastern states from Maine to Kansas, using five hundred horses and men to move performers, tents, and equipment.

Barnum had been wise in his choice of partners. Coup's expertise in advertising and transportation played an important part in the successful tour. Long before the circus arrived in each city, he had posters decorating every barn and fence within a seventy-five-mile radius. Then he arranged for excursion trains, which made special trips into the countryside and brought people to the show grounds at reduced prices.

While Coup and Costello managed the day-to-day affairs of the Great Traveling World's Fair, Barnum had his agents look for uncommon beasts and unusual people. "Ship after ship," he said, "brought me rare and valuable animals and works of art."

The giraffe's long neck always helped advertise a circus. Since no giraffe had ever lived more than two years after being brought to America, other circus managers had given up trying to import them. However, this only made Barnum more determined always to have one on hand because their scarcity made them even more valuable as curiosities. He had two sent to him and a third kept at the Zoological Gardens in London, ready to be shipped at a moment's notice. Barnum also bought several huge sea lions. They weighed a thousand pounds each and ate sixty to a hundred pounds of fish daily.

The greatest attraction of the circus, however, was a family of so-called cannibals from the Fiji Islands. According to Barnum, this people-eating tribe had been captured in war by King Thokambau. They had been rescued by one of Barnum's agents as they were about to be killed and possibly eaten themselves. After accepting a large sum of money, King Thokambau allowed him to use the cannibals in his circus. Barnum also promised that he would return the captives to the king, a promise he did not keep. The cannibals portrayed their manners and customs and performed their wild war dances for fascinated audiences everywhere.

Barnum was so successful in gathering bigger and better attractions that by its second year, the circus was too large to move from town to town using horses and wagons as other circuses did. So, Coup invented an efficient system for loading and unloading the circus from trains. He ended up using sixty freight cars, six passenger cars, and three engines. Coup also added a second ring to the circus and installed the first center pole used in a circus tent.

Crowds greeted the show everywhere it went. The circus often traveled a hundred miles in a single night in order to perform in the larger towns every day. The excursion trains brought thousands of people from fifty, seventy-five, and a hundred miles away. "Thousands more came in wagons and on horseback," Barnum said, "frequently arriving in the night and camping out." In October of 1872, the warm-weather tenting season closed in Detroit, Michigan, when the largest group of people ever assembled in that state attended the circus.

In the winter, only part of the circus traveled to the southern states. To house the rest and give employment to some two hundred people who would otherwise have been idle, Barnum bought a building in New York City. After enlarging and remodeling it, he installed his valuable collection of animals and living curiosities. The grand opening of what Barnum called his Museum, Menagerie, Hippodrome, and Circus took place on November 18, 1872.

"It was a beautiful sight," said Barnum as he recalled how the huge building was filled from the pit to the dome with an eager audience of almost three thousand people. The dazzling lights, the sweet music, and the brilliant performers captivated everyone who was there.

Four weeks later, at 4:00 A.M. on Christmas Eve, a fire was discovered in the boiler room of the structure. Except for two elephants and a camel, the building and everything in it were destroyed. This was the fourth disastrous fire that Barnum had suffered. Just as in the cases of his three previous fires, Barnum's insurance failed to cover his losses.

Without a moment's hesitation, Barnum started over. He contacted his agents in Europe and directed them to send replacements for all the animals that had been lost, no matter how much it cost. By the first week in April of 1873, just three months after the fire, Barnum and his partners placed a circus on the road that outdid any attempt ever made with a traveling show in any country.

Called Barnum's Traveling World's Fair, its expenses were five thousand dollars a day. Barnum's friends declared that he would go broke and Barnum knew that there was a limit as to how far one person could go in spending money on promoting a business. "But," he said, "I have never found that limit. My experience has been that the more a manager will provide for the public, the more likely they will respond." And the 1873 season proved his theory. Although his tents covered twice the space they had in the previous year, they were crowded with visitors.

While the circus was in Cleveland, Ohio, Barnum visited Trot, a sickly young boy. During their conversation, Trot said that he wished he could see the circus

menagerie. "If you can't go to the show," said Barnum, "we must bring the show to you."

He left, and a while later, a keeper appeared with a
drove of elephants and camels. They marched into
Trot's yard and came to a halt near his window. Then
they spent half an hour going through a special performance, doing all the tricks that Trot wanted to see.

Those who knew Barnum were not surprised
when they heard about what he had done. Barnum
loved children and wanted to make them happy.
When he attended his circus, he did not watch the
performers. He was more interested in watching the
children's reactions, waiting for them to tell him what
they thought of his show.

Everywhere he took his exhibits or his circus, he
invited orphans to attend free of charge. He said there
was "no picture so beautiful as ten thousand smiling,
bright-eyed, happy children; no music so sweet as
their clear-ringing laughter. That I have had power,
year after year, of providing innocent amusements for
the little ones, to create such pictures, to evoke such
music, is my proudest and happiest reflection."

In September of 1873, Barnum left the circus in
Coup's capable hands and sailed for Europe to rest, to
attend the International Exhibition in Vienna, Aus-
tria, and to see what new attractions he could find for
his circus. In England he met his old friend, John Fish,
and traveled throughout the country with him and his
daughter Nancy.

While Barnum was in Europe, Coup got a lease on some land owned by the Harlem Railroad on Madison Avenue and Twenty-seventh Street in New York. He erected a huge structure so he could exhibit the circus and other spectacles in a permanent building. He called it the Great Roman Hippodrome and had plans for it to be a circus, zoo, aquarium, show ring, and museum. At first, Barnum was reluctant to risk money in the venture. The panic of 1873 was in full force. Many banks closed and business was bad. People did not have much money to spend on amusements. When Coup assured him that he already had the money, Barnum joined him. Once committed, he lost no time. He visited zoological gardens, circuses, and public exhibitions all over Europe to get new ideas from other managers.

In Hamburg, Germany, he purchased a shipload of rare birds and wild animals including elephants, giraffes, and ostriches. He had just finished his business in Hamburg when he received word of the death of his wife, Charity, who had been ill for a number of years.

Barnum was overwhelmed by grief. He arranged Charity's funeral and burial by cable, then remained alone in his hotel room for many days. He returned to London and spent several quiet weeks by himself.

Chapter / Eleven

The Greatest Show
on Earth

After several weeks of mourning Charity's death, Barnum once more began to recover his unlimited zest for life. He sent his agents to Spain and Africa while he visited many European circuses and zoological gardens. He purchased the finest animals and engaged the most talented artists for the permanent circus to be housed in the Roman Hippodrome which his partner, Coup, was building. His shipments to New York included sixteen ostriches, ten elands (African antelopes), ten zebras, a team of reindeer with Lapland drivers, a troupe of performing ponies, and an assortment of monkeys and goats.

As one of its chief attractions, Sanger's Circus in London had a pageant called the "Congress of Monarchs." During this pageant, historical figures marched in a spectacular procession around the circus ring at the beginning of each show. Barnum decided to present his own version of the congress, which had been used in London for several years. He bought copies of all the equipment needed and had it shipped to America.

Barnum returned to the United States in April of 1874, one week after the opening of the Roman Hippodrome. It had been advertised as the largest amusement building ever constructed. Inside, the track running around its edge was one-fifth of a mile long and thirty feet wide. Ten thousand spectators filled the Roman Hippodrome night after night.

Every performance at the Hippodrome opened with the "Congress of Nations," which was the new name of the "Congress of Monarchs." One thousand people and several hundred horses, elephants, camels, llamas, ostriches, and other creatures paraded in a procession of golden chariots and carriages carrying actors costumed as Queen Victoria, Napoleon, the Pope, the Czar of Russia, the Emperor of China, and other historical rulers. The crowd went wild when the Stars and Stripes, Revolutionary War soldiers, and American Indians appeared at the end.

Following the historical pageant was a variety of acts: women riding English thoroughbreds, Roman chariot races, cattle-lassoing, hurdle races, elephant and camel running matches, wire-walking, and balloon flights by a man billed as Professor Donaldson. Besides all this and more, there was a magnificent menagerie of animals.

After a few months in New York, the whole Hippodrome establishment, housed in immense tents,
spent three successful weeks in Boston. From there, it
was moved by train to several other eastern cities
before returning to its New York headquarters.

At the same time, Barnum's tent show—Barnum's Great Museum, Menagerie, Circus, and Traveling World's Fair—was on the road. And Barnum
became the sole owner of both enterprises when his
partners Costello and Coup sold out to him.

Like his father before him, Barnum did not grieve
long over the death of his first wife. Ten months later,
in the autumn of 1874, he married again. Barnum had
met his second wife, Nancy Fish, in 1858 when she
was eight, and he was forty-eight. While he was lecturing in Manchester, England, Nancy's father, John
Fish, had paid him a visit. Fish and Barnum became
good friends and traveling companions. Nancy often
accompanied them.

After her marriage to Barnum, Nancy continued
to travel with him. She provided the companionship
that his wife, Charity, had not been able to give him
because of her poor health. And Barnum experienced
the joys of a childhood he felt he had missed, while he
and Nancy attended clambakes and picnics, open air
concerts in Seaside Park, and the theater and opera in
New York.

Although Barnum had reached his sixty-fourth
birthday, he continued to fill his life with endless

activities. In addition to overseeing his Hippodrome and his traveling circus, he frequently gave lectures in both the United States and England. He was again elected to the General Assembly of Connecticut.

Barnum also took part in the civic affairs of Bridgeport. There was hardly anything in the city that he was not connected with in some way. He was the first president of the Bridgeport Hospital, vice-president of the Bridgeport Board of Trade, and Trustee of the First Universalist Church. For a time, he was a stockholder and president of the Bridgeport Hydraulic Company, which supplied the city with water. He helped establish the Bridgeport Library, and its first card was issued to him. He worked toward getting a bridge built over the Pequonnock River to connect Bridgeport to East Bridgeport, and bought a street car company, which provided East Bridgeport's people with transportation by horse-drawn cars.

On April 5, 1875, Barnum was elected mayor of Bridgeport after only a week's campaign, but he was not very successful as a mayor. Long before his year in office was finished, he decided he would not run for mayor again. And he stuck to his decision.

Although Barnum concerned himself with many things, the circus was his main interest. After sending the exhibits from the Hippodrome and the circus on separate tours in 1874, Barnum decided to combine the two into one stupendous traveling show. The show, known as P.T. Barnum's New and Greatest

Show on Earth, was transported in one hundred railroad cars.

The circus now had millions of dollars worth of
exhibits. Audiences loved the six German stallions
that performed as a drill team and marched on their
hind legs. Barnum also hired Mademoiselle Zazel, the
"Human Projectile," and Captain Constantine, a
tatooed man.

Mademoiselle Zazel was, in fact, an Englishwom-
an named Rosa M. Richter. Wearing pink tights, she
was flung from a wooden cannon by a spring and flew
forty feet through the air. Her partner, hanging by his
knees from a trapeze, then caught her. Mademoiselle
Zazel was the first human cannonball in circus history.

Barnum sometimes introduced Captain Georgius
Constantine as a Greek nobleman who had been forc-
ibly tattooed all over his body by Chinese pirates in
Burma. Not a quarter inch of Captain Constantine's
skin was unmarked. From head to toe he was covered
with almost four hundred designs, mostly of wildlife.
Constantine had hired six tattoo artists for three
months to do the work.

There were many traveling shows which claimed
to be equal to Barnum's, but he outshone his rivals
completely. Some of them he bought out. Others
folded. The rest struggled along by visiting the back-
country towns.

Barnum received his first real challenge in 1880
from the Great London Circus, Sanger's Royal British

Menagerie, and Great International Allied Shows, known widely as Allied Shows. Allied Shows was owned by James E. Cooper, James Anthony Bailey, and James L. Hutchinson, and Barnum found that he had met men who offered him stiff competition. They were young and had business talent and energy equal to his own. After some discussion, the four men decided to join their two shows. Sink or swim, they would exhibit them for one admission price for at least one season. Together they built winter quarters for the combined circuses in Bridgeport. Bailey took care of the day-to-day management while Barnum continued to travel in search of new display ideas.

At first, the show was known as the Barnum and London Circus. Then, Cooper and Hutchinson sold out to the other two and the circus was renamed the Barnum and Bailey Greatest Show on Earth.

The Barnum and London Circuses opened at the original Madison Square Garden (on the same site that the Roman Hippodrome had occupied) and, for the first time, the circus had three rings. Earlier, a torchlight procession through the city had advertised this first greatest show on earth. Thousands of animals, brightly decorated circus wagons, clowns, beautiful women, acrobats, American Indians, brass bands, and a calliope (steam organ) paraded past half a million people. It was called the most brilliant display ever seen in America.

Chapter/Twelve

Well, I'm Barnum

A year after Barnum and Bailey joined forces, Barnum carried out what many consider his greatest achievement as a circus owner. Of all things connected with the circus, Barnum liked the elephants the best. And, he wanted Jumbo, an African elephant, the most famous elephant in all animal history, the most popular animal in the London zoo, and the largest one in captivity in 1882.

When he was four years old, Jumbo was captured by some Arab hunters in East Africa. He was sold to a Bavarian collector, Johann Schmidt, and in 1861, Schmidt sold him to Jardin des Plantes, the Paris zoo. He was only four feet tall when the Paris zoo traded him to the Royal Zoological Society of London for a rhinoceros.

Jumbo lived in the London zoo for seventeen years, growing to a tremendous size. He weighed thirteen thousand pounds, stood twelve feet tall at the shoulder, and had a seven-foot-long trunk which could reach twenty-six feet above the ground. He ate nearly two hundred pounds of hay a day, several bushels of grain, over a dozen loaves of bread, plus fruits, vegetables, and all the peanuts visitors gave him.

Barnum had not only seen Jumbo many times on his London visits, but he also had ridden him. Although it seemed hopeless, he told one of his agents that he would like nothing better than to obtain the giant elephant for his circus. Much to his surprise, his wish was granted in 1881. The zoo agreed to sell Jumbo to Barnum for ten thousand dollars because the superintendent was afraid that the elephant would go wild someday and cause enormous destruction. Barnum hired Matthew Scott, who had been Jumbo's keeper for twenty years, to continue with his job.

If Jumbo had been a favorite before Barnum bought him, he became the biggest celebrity in England afterward. The Royal Zoological Gardens were crowded every day by the public. England was flooded with Jumbo cigars; Jumbo earrings, fans, hats, and ties; Jumbo underclothing and Jumbo overcoats; Jumbo boots and Jumbo perfumes. Restaurants featured Jumbo soups and hash, Jumbo stews and salads, and Jumbo pies and ice cream.

The English newspapers were filled with the "Jumbo story." Engravings of Jumbo in various poses were published, and so were picture books. The music halls rang with a song about Jumbo.

A lawsuit for an order against the removal of Jumbo from England was brought to the Court of Chancery, but it was unsuccessful. Thousands of British citizens, plus Queen Victoria and the Prince of Wales, begged Barnum to reconsider. Jumbo got into the act by lying down and refusing to go into the cage built to hold him on his journey across the ocean.

None of the protests stopped Barnum. Jumbo finally was put on board a British freight steamer on March 26, 1882. After a fifteen-day voyage, he arrived in the New York harbor. Barnum, Bailey, and Hutchinson met Jumbo and his keeper, Matthew Scott, and led them up Broadway to Madison Square Garden where the circus was playing. Jumbo was frightened at first, but he soon grew accustomed to the crowds, noise, and music. Barnum reported that in just six weeks he attracted $336,000 in receipts to the circus.

On September 15, 1885, Jumbo did his usual circus act with his partner, a baby elephant named after Tom Thumb. His keeper was leading Jumbo and Tom Thumb to their private railroad car when an unscheduled special freight train seemed to appear out of nowhere. The keeper jumped to safety; Tom Thumb suffered a broken leg; Jumbo's skull was fractured and he received internal injuries. Within a few minutes he was dead.

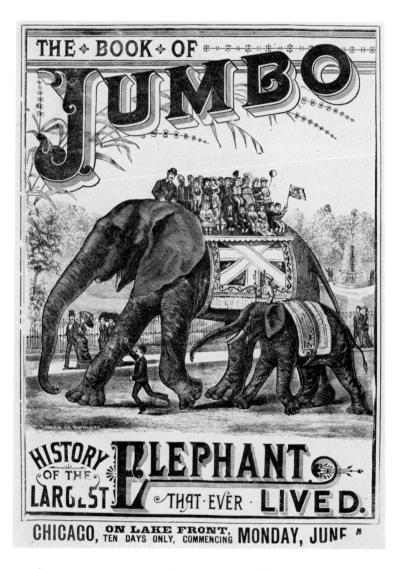

Jumbo was a star attraction of the Barnum and Bailey Greatest Show on Earth. This cover from a Barnum circus program book announces Jumbo's appearance with the circus in Chicago.

Jumbo's hide, which weighed 1,538 pounds, was placed on a shaped frame of wood and traveled with the circus for a time. Eventually, it was placed in the natural history museum at Tufts University in Medford, Massachusetts. Although the elephant has been dead over a hundred years, his name lives on today as a word used to express hugeness, as in jumbo shrimp and jumbo jet.

A few days after Jumbo's death, Barnum suggested to a publisher that he write a children's book about Jumbo's life, but nothing came of the idea. Barnum had already written one children's book in 1876 called *Lion Jack: A Story of Perilous Adventures Among Wild Men and the Capturing of Wild Beasts; Showing How Menageries Are Made.* Barnum published two more juvenile books, *Jack in the Jungle* in 1880, and *Dick Broadhead, A Tale of Perilous Adventure* in 1888. Some biographers maintain that these two books and another book said to be by Barnum, *The Wild Beasts, Birds, and Reptiles of the World, the Story of Their Capture,* were written by a press agent of the circus for Barnum.

There is no doubt, however, that Barnum is the author of *The Humbugs of the World,* published in 1866, in which he discusses fake lotteries, fortune-tellers, phony mining stocks, and other fraudulent schemes. It is certain that Barnum also wrote the pamphlet *Why I Am A Universalist* in 1895, and the several versions of his autobiography.

In 1886 and 1887, the Barnum and Bailey Greatest Show on Earth visited over three hundred cities and traveled over twenty thousand miles. Then in November of 1887, Barnum suffered another fire, his fifth. The circus's winter quarters at Bridgeport were destroyed. Only thirty elephants and one lion escaped.

Barnum was now seventy-seven years old. The fire loss reached $250,000, and, as usual, Barnum was underinsured at $30,000. People thought he would give up show business altogether. But he and Bailey immediately began to rebuild. By the following spring, they opened with an even bigger circus than they had had before the fire.

Barnum realized that he was growing older, but he treated the approaching end with the same optimism he had treated everything in life. Barnum had become a millionaire many times over. He had earned a rest, but he still was not ready for retirement. He had spent his life spreading joy and excitement. The people of the United States had enjoyed his circus for twenty years. Now he felt it was time to take it to London.

In the winter of 1889, Bailey packed up the show and he and Barnum took it to the huge Olympia arena in London. It was the biggest show in circus history and a smashing success. All of his friends attended. Queen Victoria, entering her seventies, sat in the royal box with the Prince of Wales. The Princess of Wales attended four times.

Going to the circus became the "fashion" in London. Almost everyone from the nobility attended. The fifteen thousand seat amusement building was crowded at every performance. Midway through each show, Barnum entered the arena in his carriage. Performers and the people in the audience greeted him with a standing ovation and ear-splitting cheers. He doffed his silk hat, bowed, and announced, "I suppose you all came to see Barnum. Well, I'm Barnum." There were more cheers as he left. Then it was on with the show.

When Barnum and his wife returned home in March of the following year, they moved into Marina, the fourth and last home Barnum built in Bridgeport. Marina was erected about three feet east of Waldemere, which had grown too big and expensive for a family of just two. Waldemere was then split into three houses and hauled away to three different locations. The cellar was filled in and sodded. Barnum had built Marina especially for Nancy, and when the house was finished, he presented her with its deed.

Although the London trip had been hard on Barnum's heart, which had been weak for some years, his family gathered to celebrate his eightieth birthday on July 4, 1890. Then Barnum and Nancy spent August in the Adirondack Mountains, as had been their custom for many years. They returned to Marina for a short time before they traveled to Colorado. Along the way they stopped in Kansas, where Barnum saw his Greatest Show on Earth for the last time. He told

Nancy that he had never enjoyed a journey more. "He was perfectly and exuberantly happy," she said, "thinking all the world fair, and all mankind true. No less happy was the coming home. . .to Marina."

Soon after returning home, Barnum suffered what the doctors called an "acute congestion of the brain." Although he recovered somewhat, this was the beginning of his last sickness. From then until his death, he continued to carry on his business affairs. Among other things, he made plans for providing a unique, domed brownstone-and-brick building to house the Bridgeport Scientific, Historical, and Medical Societies, now known as the Barnum Institute of Science and History. He also gave thirty thousand dollars to the natural history museum at Tufts University.

His wife said that Barnum did not suffer a great deal in his last illness. He was always cheerful, often merry. "His room was the one bright spot in a sad house," she said, "and his hearty laugh was often heard."

And he still enjoyed a good joke. One evening the doctor told him he might have rice, milk, and a little fruit for his meals. The next day, when the doctor asked what he had eaten, Barnum replied, "I followed your advice. I took rice and milk and two hard-boiled eggs."

"What?" cried the doctor.

"They *are* hen fruit, you know!" said Barnum.

Although he would not speak of his own death, he spoke of death in general, saying, "It is a good thing, a beautiful thing, just as much so as life; and it is wrong to grieve about it and to look on it as an evil."

Like a skyrocket, Barnum had dazzled the crowds again and again with great bursts of fiery color. With the circus in London, the last brilliant charge had exploded. Then one by one the lingering sparks flickered out until the last one disappeared on April 8, 1891. Phineas Taylor Barnum was dead. But his memory will linger as long as there is a circus.

Bibliography

Barnum, Nancy Fish. *The Last Chapter: In Memorium P.T. Barnum.* Privately printed, 1891.

Barnum, Phineas Taylor. *Dollars and Sense, or How to Get On.* Chicago: Eastern Publishing House, 1890.

————. *Life of P.T. Barnum Written By Himself.* First edition, New York: Samson Law, 1855. Revised and published in various editions under this title until 1890.

————. *Struggles and Triumphs, or Forty Years' Recollections of P.T. Barnum Written By Himself,* with additions and revisions. New York: American News Company, 1871.

————. *The Humbugs of the World.* New York: John Camden Hotten, 1866.

Bradford, Gamaliel. *Damaged Souls.* Boston: Houghton Mifflin, 1923.

Harris, Neil. *Humbug: The Art of P.T. Barnum.* Boston: Little, 1973.

Finley, Ruth E. *The Lady of Godey's—Sarah Josepha Hale.* Philadelphia: J.B. Lippincott Company, 1931.

Root, Harvey W. *The Unknown Barnum.* New York: Harper and Brothers, 1927.

Rourke, Constance Mayfield. *Trumpets of Jubilee.* New York: J. Cape, 1927.

Wallace, Irving. *The Fabulous Showman: The Life and Times of P.T. Barnum.* New York: Knopf, 1959.

Werner, M.R. *Barnum.* New York: Harcourt, Brace and Company, 1923.

Index

0732-90

921
BARNUM   Tompert, Ann

         The greatest
         showman on earth

DATE DUE

BRODART	02/90	11.95
FE 18 '93		
MR 4 '93		
MR 18		